Ultramarathon Man

Ultramarathon Man

Confessions of an All-Night Runner

DEAN KARNAZES

JEREMY P. TARCHER/PENGUIN
A MEMBER OF PENGUIN GROUP (USA) INC.
NEW YORK

JEREMY P. TARCHER/PENGUIN
Published by the Penguin Group
www.penguin.com
Penguin Group (USA) Inc., 375 Hudson Street, New York, New York 10014, USA ·
Penguin Group (Canada), 10 Alcorn Avenue, Toronto, Ontario, Canada M4V 3B2
(a division of Pearson Penguin Canada Inc.) · Penguin Books Ltd, 80 Strand, London
WC2R 0RL, England · Penguin Ireland, 25 St Stephen's Green, Dublin 2, Ireland
(a division of Penguin Books Ltd) · Penguin Group (Australia), 250 Camberwell Road,
Camberwell, Victoria 3124, Australia (a division of Pearson Australia Group Pty Ltd) ·
Penguin Books India Pvt Ltd, 11 Community Centre, Panchsheel Park, New Delhi –
110 017, India · Penguin Group (NZ), Cnr Airborne and Rosedale Roads, Albany,
Auckland 1310, New Zealand (a division of Pearson New Zealand Ltd) · Penguin Books
(South Africa) (Pty) Ltd, 24 Sturdee Avenue, Rosebank, Johannesburg 2196, South Africa

Penguin Books Ltd, Registered Offices: 80 Strand, London WC2R 0RL, England

Most Tarcher/Penguin books are available at special quantity discounts for bulk
purchase for sales promotions, premiums, fund-raising, and educational needs. Special
books or book excerpts also can be created to fit specific needs. For details, write
Penguin Group (USA) Inc. Special Markets, 375 Hudson Street, New York, NY 10014.

Library of Congress Cataloging-in-Publication Data

Karnazes, Dean, date.
    Ultramarathon man / Dean Karnazes.
    p. cm.
    ISBN 1-58542-278-9
        1. Karnazes, Dean, date.   2. Runners (Sports)—United States—Biography.
3. Running races.   4. Endurance sports.   I. Title.
GV1061.15.K39A3   2005   2004051607
796.42'092—dc22
[B]

Printed in the United States of America
10   9   8   7   6   5   4   3   2   1

This book is printed on acid-free paper. ∞

Book design by Lovedog Studio

*This book is dedicated
to my sister, Pary,
who always encouraged
me to follow my heart.*

Contents

Part One

Chapter 1

The Long Road to Santa Cruz

Sleep is for wimps.

—Christopher Gaylord,
underground ultra-endurance legend

Napa Valley, California
Friday evening, September 29, 2000

It was approaching midnight as I wove up the deserted road, wearing nothing more than a pair of shorts and a sleeveless vest, a cell phone tucked in a pocket of my pack. It had been hours since I'd last had contact with humanity, and the night air was silent and warm. By the light of the full moon, I could see grapevines along my path and hear them rustle in the breeze. But I wasn't fully appreciating the view; I kept thinking about food. I was famished. Earlier tonight, I'd eaten a bowl of maca-roni and cheese, a large bag of pretzels, two bananas, a PowerBar, and a chocolate éclair. But that was more than three hours ago. On big occasions like this one, I needed more food. And I needed it *now*.

At less than 5 percent body fat, my body is ripped like a prizefighter's, nothing left to shed. My diet is strict—high protein, good fats, no refined sugar, only slowly metabolized carbs—but tonight I had to be reckless. Without massive caloric binges—burgers, french fries, ice cream, pies and cakes—my metabolism would come to a screeching halt and I'd be unable to accomplish my mission.

Right now, it craved a big, greasy pizza.

The problem was, I hadn't had access to food in the past few hours. I was heading west through the remote outskirts of Sonoma, well off the beaten path, no food in sight. Proceeding farther from civilization, I'd watched the signal indicator on my cell phone diminish to the point of no reception, severing my contact with the out-side world. Midnight was nearing, and I was ravaged.

The night air was dry and fresh, and, despite my hunger, I was able to enjoy the tranquillity of the sur-roundings. It was a rare moment of serenity in an other-wise frenetic life. At times I found myself mesmerized by the full moon illuminating the hillsides.

At others all I could think about was finding the next 7-Eleven.

When I left the office early today, I received backslaps and hoots of encouragement from several co-workers, most of whom are aware of my *other* life. One minute I was all business, discussing revenue forecasts and corporate strategy in my neatly pressed Friday casuals. The next I was jamming out the door like a wired teenager, psyched about the upcoming weekend festivities. I'd learned to switch from work mode to play mode in the span of several paces. I liked my job plenty, but I *loved* what I was about to do.

At 5:00 P.M., I pushed a button on my stopwatch and the mission was afoot, so to speak. It started in the bucolic little town of Calistoga at the northern reaches of the Napa Valley. The afternoon was warm and cloudless as the townsfolk milled about stoically. One guy tipped his hat and said "Howdy" as I passed, and a lady sweeping the sidewalk with a reed broom stopped and smiled. They were friendly enough, though judging from the peculiar looks I received it was clear I was being sized up: *We know he's not here to cause trouble, but what, exactly, is he doing?*

Alongside me in our VW campervan (aka the Mother Ship) was my family: my parents, my wife, Julie, and our two kids, Alexandria and Nicholas. The Mother Ship would be our operational "brain center" for the next three days. That, however, implies a level of sleekness that didn't exist. The Mother Ship was more like a roaming funhouse, cluttered with maps, toys, travel magazines, binoculars, and homemade bug-catching jars. Between the seats were pieces of Fig Newtons and stale Goldfish dusted with beach sand. It was the perfect anti–feng shui environment, and we loved it.

Macaroni and cheese from a box was easy to cook on the Mother Ship's small stove, and that's what we'd had for dinner tonight. Because of my two lives, we didn't eat together as a family as often as I liked, so I treasured this meal—dehydrated cheese or not.

We were like any other happy family having dinner together, only we were sitting on the guardrail on the side of a highway. The kids didn't seem to find it strange—they didn't know any different, really—and my parents had grown accustomed to sipping wine from a paper cup while balancing on the narrow railing as cars whizzed by. There wasn't too much traffic on the road tonight, so we engaged in pleasant dinner conversation.

I had seconds and thirds, and then I finished the rest of my wife's meal. Dessert followed: two bananas, a PowerBar, and a chocolate éclair.

"I hate to dine and ditch," I said, not pausing long enough to sit down, "but I've got to be moving along."

"Daddy, are you going to be gone all night again?" my daughter Alexandria asked. Her big brown eyes filled with enthusiastic curiosity, as if trying to understand why her daddy had this odd yearning that wasn't shared by many other daddies.

"Yes, sweetie, I am. But we'll have breakfast together tomorrow morning."

Although that conversation was just a few hours ago, it now seemed like a long time back. Nearing midnight, they would now all be happily asleep inside the Mother Ship as I made my way through Sonoma and continued west toward the town of Petaluma.

Known for its thrift stores and bowling alleys, Petaluma isn't a bustling metropolis. But to its credit, the town does have a Round Table Pizza, one of the greatest franchises on the planet.

You see, other pizza companies are not as flexible as Round Table. Most of them have complicated delivery rules and policies—picky little things like requiring you to provide a street address in order to have a pizza delivered. Imagine that—you actually have to tell them exactly where you are! Round Table, on the other hand, will deliver a pizza to just about anywhere.

Over the years, I've pushed the envelope with Round Table, and they've consistently outperformed all other pizza chains. I was so confident in their pizza-delivering prowess that I once even had them bring one to my house.

Cresting the peak and seeing that my cell phone now had service, I dialed. The signal was weak.

"Round Table," a young voice answered. Loud rock music blared in the background.

"I need to order a pizza."

"What's that? You need a pizza?"

Why else would anybody be calling the Round Table delivery line? *"YES, I NEED TO ORDER A PIZZA! I NEED PIZZA!"*

"Okay, dude, no need to scream."

"Sorry."

"That's all right. I know how edgy people get about their pizza."

"I'm not edgy, I'm just hungry," I said in a very edgy tone.

"Whatever, dude. Just be assured that we're going to get you the tastiest grinds imaginable. I'm the manager. Now what's it gonna be?"

"I'll take the Hawaiian style, with extra cheese. Extra olives. Extra ham. Oh yeah . . . extra pineapple, too."

"Extra everything? I'll throw it all on there. What size you after?"

This was a tricky question. I didn't have the means to carry any uneaten portions, but if I ordered too little, I'd run out of fuel and never reach Marin before sunrise.

"How many does a large feed?"

"Five, with all those extras. How many in your party?"

"It's just me. I'll take the large."

"Cannonball, dude! You must be operating on some kind of hunger."

If you only knew, I thought. "Do you have dessert?"

"Cherry cheesecake. It's killer—I tested some earlier tonight."

"Okay, I'll have one."

"One slice?"

"No, I want the whole damn thing."

"Dude, this is epic!"

"How long do you think it'll take?"

"Twenty, thirty minutes. You in some kind of rush?"

"No rush, really, I'll be out here a while. I just need to know how long it'll take so I can to tell you where to meet me."

"Okay . . . I guess. Let's say twenty-five minutes."

"Then I'll meet you at the corner of Highway 116 and Arnold Drive."

"What, right on the corner?" he asked. "That's a pretty lonely stretch of highway. What color's your car?"

"I'm not in a car," I said. "But I'll be easy to spot. I'm the only one out here running."

"Running?" There was a brief moment of silence. "Is someone chasing you?"

"No," I laughed.

"But it's midnight!" he said.

"Yes, it's late. And that's why I need pizza. I'm starving."

"Got it." [Long pause.] "Makes perfect sense. Is there anything else I can bring you?"

"Is there a Starbucks in town?"

"Yeah, but I'm sure they're closed by now. But I've got my own stash of beans right here. I'll brew some up while the pizza's cooking. You just keep running straight on Highway 116 and we'll track you down."

After giving him my cell number and hanging up, I

put my head down and kept plowing into the darkness. If they were going to locate me along the route, there was no need to wait on the corner, which was a good thing. Standing idle in the evening air was a sure way to invite a debilitating leg cramp.

Replacing my cell phone in the back pocket of my pack, I pulled out the picture of a little girl. Even with tubes and needles stuck all over her body, her face looked vibrant. But she *was* sick; in fact, she was near death, and I was running to help save her. I took one final look at the picture and tucked it carefully away again.

Exactly twenty-five minutes later, a dusty pickup truck with oversized tires came barreling down the road. My pizza had arrived. To my surprise, the young manager was behind the wheel.

"Dude!" he cried, jumping out of the car. "You're mad. This is awesome!"

He pulled the pizza off the passenger seat and opened the box. It was masterfully crafted, almost as high as it was wide, with lots of pineapple and olives piled on top. It looked like something you'd feed a rhinoceros. I paid the tab, thanked him, and prepared to charge on.

"You're gonna keep running?" he asked. "Don't you want a lift?"

"Now that I've got some fuel," I answered, holding up the food, "I'm going to put it to good use."

"But how far are you gonna go?"

"I'm headed to the beach," I said.

"To the beach!" he cried. "Dude, Bodega Bay's at least thirty miles from here!"

Actually, I was heading to the beach in Santa Cruz—over 150 miles from here—but I didn't think either of us was prepared to face up to that reality.

"I can't believe it's humanly possible to run thirty miles," he gasped. "Are you like Carl Lewis or something?"

"Ah . . . yeah," I replied. "I'm like Carl Lewis, only slower."

"Where will you sleep?"

"I won't."

"You're running straight through the night? This is insane. I love it!" He jumped back in his truck. "I can't wait to tell the guys back at the shop." He sped off.

I liked this kid. To most non-runners, running is at best boring and at worst terribly painful and senseless. But he seemed genuinely intrigued by the venture, and we'd connected on an almost primal level, though I didn't sense he'd take up the sport anytime soon.

With the cheesecake stacked on top of the pizza, I started running again, eating as I went. Over the years I'd perfected the craft of eating on the fly. I balanced the box of pizza and cheesecake in one hand and ate with the other. It was a good upper-body workout. Fortunately my forearms were well developed and had no problem supporting the added weight. For efficiency, I rolled four pieces of pizza into one big log like a huge Italian burrito. Easier to fit it in my mouth that way.

Just as I was finishing this first course, I heard the manager's truck approaching again. The loose muffler was a dead giveaway. He'd forgotten to give me the coffee. We filled one of my water bottles with the dark brew and I drank the rest. I tried to pay him for it, but he wouldn't take any money.

As he was about to drive away again, the young man tilted his head out of the truck window and asked, "So dude, do you mind me asking *why* you're doing this?"

Where to begin? "Oh man," I replied, "I'll have to get back to you on that one."

And now's the time to ponder his question. Millions of Americans run. They run for the exercise, for their cardiovascular health, for the endorphin high. In 2003, a record-setting 460,000 people completed one of the country's many marathons. They pushed the outer limits of their endurance to complete the 26.2 miles.

Then there's the small hardcore group of runners, a kind of runners' underground, who are called ultramarathoners. For us, a marathon is just a warm-up. We run 50-mile races, 100-mile races. We'll run twenty-four hours and more without sleep, barely pausing for food and water, or even to use the bathroom. We run up and down mountains; through Death Valley in the dead of summer; at the South Pole. We push our bodies, minds, and spirits well past what most humans would consider the limits of pain and exertion.

I'm one of the few who's run beyond 100 miles without resting, which I guess makes me an extra-ultramarathoner. Or just nuts. Whenever people hear that I've run 100 miles at a clip, they inevitably ask two questions. The first is "How can you do that?" The second, and much harder to answer, is the same one that pizza guy asked me: *"Why?"*

It's an excellent question, though addictions are never neatly defined. When asked why he was attempting to be the first to climb Mount Everest, George Mallory offered the famously laconic, "Because it's there." That seems to satisfy people enough for it to have become a famous adage. But it's really not much of an answer. Still, I can understand Mallory's clipped response. When people ask me why I run such improbable distances for nights on end, I've often been tempted to answer with something like, "Because I can." It's true as far as it goes, and athletes aren't always the most introspective souls. But it's not a complete answer. It's not even satisfying to me. I've got questions of my own.

What am I running from?

Who am I running for?

Where I am running to?

Every runner has a story. Here's mine.

Chapter 2

The Formative Years

Of all the animals, the boy is the most unmanageable.

—Plato

Los Angeles
1969–1976

I've been running much of my life. I grew up the oldest of three kids. My brother Kraig is a year younger than I am, and my sister Pary came along two years after him.

Some of my earliest memories are of running home from kindergarten. We were a working-class family living in Los Angeles, and my father worked two jobs to make ends meet. I didn't want to burden my mother with getting me home from school every day, so I started running.

At first, my route was the most direct path from the school back to our house. In time, however, I began to invent diversionary routes that would extend the run and take me through uncharted territory and new neighborhoods. Running home from school became more enjoyable than attending it. Running gave me a sense of freedom and exploration that school never did. School was about sitting still and trying to behave as someone explained what the world was like. Running was about going out and experiencing it firsthand. I watched buildings go up, witnessed the birds migrating south, saw the leaves falling and the days shortening as the seasons changed. No textbook could compare to this real-life lesson.

By the third grade, I was participating in organized running events (some of which I organized myself). The distances were short, often only the length of a football field. Sometimes it was hard finding other kids to run with, and I found myself constantly campaigning for classmates to join me. My relatives from the Old Country frequently reminded me that the Greeks were great runners. The marathon, after all, was conceived in Greece.

"Constantine," they would say, using my given name, "you will be a great Greek runner, just like your ancestors." Then they would down another round of ouzo and seal my fate with a collective *"Oppa!"*

Never mind that Pheidippides, the Greek runner who ran from the Plain of Marathon to Athens with the news that the Athenians had defeated the Persians, dropped dead from exhaustion after delivering his message. That part of the story never got mentioned.

As I grew older, I became more passionate about pushing my small body to extremes. Advancing the limits of personal endurance seemed part of my hardwiring; I found it difficult to do anything physical in moderation. By age eleven I had already trekked rim-to-rim-to-rim across the Grand Canyon, a weeklong journey carrying all my supplies on my back, and had climbed to the top of Mount Whitney, the highest mountain in the contiguous United States.

For my twelfth birthday, I wanted to celebrate with my grandparents, but they lived more than forty miles away. Not wanting to burden my folks to drive me there, I decided to ride my bike. I had no idea how to get to my grandparents' house. But I didn't let that dampen my sense of adventure. I tried to talk Kraig into joining me, but there was absolutely no way. Even a bribe with allowance money didn't work. So I stuffed the money in my pocket, told my mother I was going to the local mall, and set a course for Pasadena.

I got a lot of confused and worried looks when I asked for directions.

"That's gotta be over forty miles from here," one gas station attendant told me.

"Which way do I go?" I asked.

"You can get on this freeway and go to the 210 North, I think," he replied doubtfully.

Of course, I couldn't ride my bicycle on the freeway. I'd need to take surface streets.

"Are you sure you don't want to call your parents?" he asked.

"That's okay," I said nonchalantly, pointing at the freeway. "So you think Pasadena is that way?"

He nodded, though not with a great deal of conviction.

"Thanks," I smiled, and set a course for the closest surface street in the direction he had indicated. This was going to be good.

Ten hours later, I arrived in Pasadena. The course I'd followed meandered haphazardly through the Los Angeles basin, and there was no telling how many miles I'd covered along the way. I stopped a couple times at other service stations to ask for directions, and also to buy a soda and use the restroom. My money was entirely depleted, but that didn't matter. What mattered was that I made it to Pasadena. Now what?

I didn't know the name of my grandparents' street, or their phone number. In fact, they didn't even live in Pasadena, but in nearby San Marino. But after some wandering around, I recognized a familiar landmark— The Galley, a large ship on the corner of an intersection that had been converted into a fish-and-chips joint. We had eaten there many times, and I knew the way to my grandparents' house from there. It was about five miles from The Galley to San Marino.

Riding up their driveway, covered in black road grime, I felt a grand sense of accomplishment. I just as well could have been standing atop Mount Everest, or the moon. It was my best birthday ever.

Luckily they were home, and were both delighted, and mortified, to see me. We called my mom and dad, who were relieved to know I was safe. They weren't upset, just thankful that I was okay. Nobody ever explained to me that what I had done was dangerous. I think they were too shocked to reprimand me. And, I hoped, they were actually proud of me. My grandparents put my bicycle in the trunk of their car and drove me home. We were greeted by the entire family—a birthday party with cousins, aunts, uncles, and many neighbors. There was music and dancing, plenty of food, and ample drink for the older folks.

The conversation at the party kept coming back to my adventure. For a kid my age to do what I had just done was almost unthinkable, and I could feel the power in it, the ability to inspire. All I needed to do was get on a bike or start running for some extraordinary distance, and the family would join together and rally around me in celebration. Naive as that may seem, it's the lesson I took away on that day.

As we grew older, Kraig became convinced that my behavior was excessive. Being the middle child, he was prone to cynicism, and, in my case—given that the centerpiece of my weekend usually revolved around some extreme adventure—his feelings were probably justified. Pary, on the other hand, seemed to appreciate my peculiarities and always encouraged me to follow my passion, regardless of how strange it seemed.

"If running makes you happy, keep going," she once said to me. She was like that—even as a kid, she was heartening.

Running did make me happy, so I kept going, right into junior high, where I met my first mentor and learned more about the odd appeal of long-distance running.

Rumor was that as a young enlisted man, Jack McTavish could do more push-ups, sit-ups, and pull-ups than anyone in his platoon, officers included. And he could do them faster. Other recruits feared being paired with him; his strength and focus left them shamed. His approach to life was straightforward: he would rise earlier, train harder, and stay longer than anyone else. On those days when he didn't feel like giving 100 percent, he forced himself to give 120.

This bullheaded drive and discipline served him well as a military man. But as my junior high school track coach, I found his approach intimidating. I don't think many of the other students, or faculty members for that matter, really knew what to make of him. It was Southern California in the seventies, and he was slightly out of place. The other teachers wore puka shells, tie-dyed shirts, and long, scraggly hair. McTavish kept his hair in a tight crew cut. He wore the same outfit every day, regardless of the season or the setting: gray gym shorts, a perfectly pressed white V-neck T-shirt, and black midtop gym shoes. He always looked freshly shaven and neatly groomed. At five-feet-seven, one hundred fifty-five pounds, he was built as solidly as a tree trunk. There wasn't an ounce of fat on the man. He was cut like an inverted pear.

Coach McTavish didn't speak much, and when he did it was direct and to the point. Idle chatter was out of the question.

I met Coach for the first time outside the men's locker room, where he was doing sit-ups on the concrete floor. He stood, gave me a crushing handshake, introduced himself while looking me squarely in the eyes, then got right back into the sit-ups, hardly missing a beat.

All of us on the track team were seventh- and eighth-grade boys, but Coach always referred to us as men. There were two kinds of people in his view of the world: those he took orders from, and those he gave orders to. We were happy to obey.

Coach's approach to running didn't come out of any textbook; he simply instructed us to run as fast as we could until we crossed the finish line. Words of advice and encouragement were few and far between. His most frequent instruction to me was, "Go out harder."

Once I tried to explain that if I started faster, I would have less kick left at the end.

"Nonsense," he replied. "Go out harder *and* finish harder."

That was one of the few complete sentences Coach ever spoke to me. In two years, we probably exchanged fewer than fifty words. And of all the runners on the team, he spoke to me the most, as though I held some promise and could do right by him.

He always had my full attention. There was something strangely appealing about his balls-to-the-wall training technique, and I came to respect, even enjoy, the practice of pushing my body to the brink of collapse. The theory was simple: Whoever was willing to run the hardest, train the longest, and suffer the most would earn the spoils of victory.

At the season-end California State Long-Distance Championship, a prestigious affair held on the legendary Mount Sac track, Coach issued his dictum: "Go out harder than those other chumps," he said. And then he walked away.

All the other schools seemed to know what they were doing. Their runners wore matching, neatly tailored tracksuits that shimmered in the morning sun. They were doing wind sprints and stretches, then quietly consulting with their coaches as though they were in complete control of the situation. Our school wore the same thing as Coach, gray gym shorts and white V-neck T-shirts.

I stood on that starting line, shivering with anxiety. I thought the other runners around me knew things I didn't about how to train better and go faster. I was scared. But the mile was my event. It was the longest race in junior high, and the most physically punishing. Even without a formal running strategy, I could endure more pain than anybody. That much I was sure of. No one, I was certain, had worked as hard as I had, or was willing to push as hard as I was about to push.

The gun went off and I did exactly as Coach had instructed: I went out as hard as I possibly could. I ran as though I were in a sprint rather than a one-mile race. The aggressive start put me immediately in the lead, and I maintained a blistering pace that broadened the distance between me and the rest of the pack as the race progressed. I ran faster and faster, and my lead increased. When I broke the finish tape in first place I was so focused that I kept right on running until I noticed that people were waving at me to stop.

As I stood doubled over, trying to catch my breath, runners and coaches kept coming over to congratulate me. They said things like, "I've never seen anyone go out like that." Clearly they were taken aback by my raw determination. It was more like complete tunnel vision.

Eventually, after everyone else had walked away, Coach casually strolled up.

"Good work, son," he said. "How'd it feel?"

I was shocked. Coach had never asked me a question before.

"Well," I answered slowly, "going out hard was the right thing to do. It felt pretty good."

Coach kicked some dirt around with his foot. "If it felt *good*," he said, squinting like Clint Eastwood, "you didn't push hard enough. It's supposed to hurt like hell."

My dad got transferred and my family moved to another city a week after that race. Those were the last words Coach said to me, and I live by them to this day: If it comes easy, if it doesn't require extraordinary effort, you're not pushing hard enough: *It's supposed to hurt like hell.*

Chapter 3

Run with Your Heart

He who suffers remembers.

—Fortune cookie

Southern California
1976–1977

My family relocated from the Los Angeles area to San Clemente, a lovely little beach town at the far reaches of Southern California best known as the home of Richard Nixon's Western White House. My friend's dad headed Nixon's Secret Service detail and let us walk through the compound to get to the best surf spots. Occasionally, the ex-President would drive by in his Rolls-Royce golf cart. "How's the water today, boys?" he'd ask. "Good, Mr. President," we'd answer and, surf-

High school freshman

boards under our arms, leave it at that. No need to shoot the breeze with Nixon when the surfing was so great.

As much as I surfed, I still loved to run. So when try-outs for the cross-country team rolled around, I was raring to go. What I quickly discovered is that high school running was divided into two camps: those who ran *cross-country,* and those who ran *track.* There was a clear distinction. The kind of runner you were largely mirrored your approach to life. The cross-country guys thought the track runners were high-strung and prissy, while the track guys viewed the cross-country guys as a bunch of athletic misfits.

It's true that the guys on the cross-country team were a motley bunch. Solidly built with long, unkempt hair and rarely shaven faces, they looked more like a bunch of lumberjacks than runners. They wore baggy shorts, bushy wool socks, and furry beanie caps, even when it was roasting hot outside. Clothing rarely matched.

Track runners were tall and lanky; they were sprinters with skinny long legs and narrow shoulders. They wore long white socks, matching jerseys, and shorts that were so high that their butt-cheeks were exposed. They always appeared neatly groomed, even after running.

The cross-country guys hung out in late-night coffee shops and read books by Kafka and Kerouac. They rarely talked about running; it was just something they did. The track guys, on the other hand, were obsessed. Speed was all they ever talked about. "Think we're doing tempo work today?" they would ask each other in the hall. "Did you clock your splits on Monday?" Track members seldom stayed out past 8:00 P.M., even on weekends. They spent an inordinate amount of time shaking their limbs and loosening up. They stretched before, during, and after practice, not to mention during lunch break and assembly, and before and after using the head. The cross-country guys, on the other hand, never stretched at all.

The track guys ran intervals and kept logbooks detailing their mileage. They wore fancy watches that counted laps and recorded each lap-time. The mile was divided into four quarters, each quarter-mile split being logged and compared to previous benchmarks. Everything was measured, dissected, and evaluated.

Cross-country guys didn't take notes. They just found a trail and ran on it. Sometimes the runs would last for an hour, sometimes three. It all depended on how they felt that day. After the run they would move on to the next thing, which was usually surfing.

I gravitated toward the cross-country team, partly because I loved to surf, but mostly because the culture suited me. During my interviews with the coaches and captains of both teams, the differences were obvious. The track team was cliquish and hierarchical. I felt like I was being interrogated and examined. The cross-country team, on the other hand, seemed to be about working together. They ran for the good of the team rather than for personal gain. One runner might cover for another's weakness, so both would hang together through the low points of a run rather than trying to "drop" each other.

The track coach, Mr. Bilderback, was abrasive and domineering. During my interview, he made several off-hand remarks about the cross-country team that seemed to cross the line from a healthy rivalry to outright jealousy. The cross-country coach, Benner Cummings, insisted that I call him Benner, unlike the track coach, who didn't seem satisfied with me calling him anything short of God. Benner talked with me instead of down to me.

He was short, maybe five-feet-six, and energetic for a man in his sixties. He had an infectious smile and a full head of naturally dark hair. His skin was radiant and smooth, and he had large, fluffy eyebrows that moved as he talked.

For high school kids to respect anyone, let alone a teacher, is unusual, but every single member of our team respected Benner. He functioned more as a guru than a coach, using training methods that were unorthodox but indisputably effective. Year after year, his cross-country team placed at or near the top of the league.

Benner himself was a terrific runner who liked nothing more than to work out with his team. He frequently had us run the mile from the high school to the beach, where we'd stash our shoes in the bushes and run barefoot along the seashore. Growing up in Southern California has its advantages. Sometimes we'd run single-file in the soft sand, following each other's footsteps and rotating the front-runner at every lifeguard tower. Other times we'd mix it up, running side by side in groups of two and three.

My favorite beach training run was "chasing the tide." This was Benner's answer to wind sprints, which the track runners did obsessively with a stopwatch on hundred-meter straightaways. Our routine consisted of running along the waterline and chasing the water down as it receded, and then running away from the water as the waves washed back in, staying just inches from the tide line. We would do this for miles and miles, hardly noticing how physically demanding it was because we were so caught up in the natural rhythm of the game.

Most of the cross-country guys ran in baggy surf trunks. This was a marked departure from the traditional running shorts with their tight internal jockstrap. One of my teammates told me that he preferred wearing loose-fitting surf trunks because "the boys appreciate the fresh air." This made sense, so I adopted the practice.

Cross-country was, in many ways, a paradox. Though our approach to running may have seemed nonchalant, we still took winning seriously. If we won, our unconventional methods and beach escapades would be viewed as brilliant training tactics. If we lost, we'd be considered a bunch of freaks.

After the workout, we'd always go for a swim. Benner loved to swim. Actually, he loved to float. He would swim out past the breakers, roll onto his back, close his eyes, and hang out for an eternity. Some of us thought that he napped while floating.

It was an exciting time to be a runner. Running was experiencing a huge spike in popularity, and Nike forever changed the sport with the introduction of the first air-sole cushioning system. The waffle tread had been the gold standard in trainers, but air-sole technology ushered in a whole new level of comfort and pizzazz. I remember my first pair of Tailwinds like I remember my first crush, the way they felt in my hand, the smell of the rubberized outsoles. Watching *Gilligan's Island* reruns in the evening, I'd spend the entire episode twisting and crunching the shoes to break them in.

In junior high, the long-distance course had been one mile; in high school it was 2. 5 to 3, so I had to quickly improve my stamina and endurance. My build was far from ideal for a runner, compact and stocky rather than lean and tall. What I lacked in archetypal runner physique, however, I compensated for with a resolve to work harder than anyone else. I was always first to arrive at practice and last to leave, and I frequently didn't get home until after dark, which was just fine with me—both my parents now worked, and they got home late as well.

As the season progressed, my hard work began to pay off. My finishing times were consistently at the front of the pack, and I even won an event or two. My teammates began referring to me affectionately as "Karno," and a spirited camaraderie developed among us.

The culmination of cross-country season was the league finals. Our school was locked in a three-way tie with Mission Viejo and Laguna Beach. Adding to the pressure, Benner announced that he would be retiring as cross-country coach after this season. We would be his last team, and we wanted to make sure he ended his career with a championship.

Benner asked me to race on the varsity team for the finals, even though I was just a freshman. I accepted this invitation with honor, even though it meant I would be racing against much older and stronger runners. Some of my classmates thought I was blowing it by forgoing the possibility of winning the freshman league finals only to likely finish mid-pack in varsity. The cross-country guys, on the other hand, seemed to respect my sacrifice for a higher cause, the Team.

The event fell on a Saturday morning that was unusually cold and foggy for Southern California. My dad, who had once been an accomplished high school runner himself (albeit as a sprinter, the quarter mile being his specialty), dropped me off at the UC Irvine outdoor field. He had followed the progress of our team throughout the season, though the poor guy was commuting three hours a day and didn't always have time for all the details. Dad did know that I loved Benner's creative coaching techniques and that I put Benner and the rest of the team on a pedestal.

Our team joined together, as usual, in our little "pod" where we'd spread out beach blankets and lie around like a pack of wolves before the race began. Sometimes we'd tell jokes and have a laugh, other times we'd just stare up at the sky. That morning we told stories about

Benner. My favorite was about the time Benner showed up late to a staff meeting that was being chaired by Bilderback, the track coach. Benner quietly slipped in the back door and took a seat. His appearance was disheveled and his face was flushed. Bilderback stopped the meeting and inquired, in front of the entire staff, why Benner was late.

Benner lived on the far side of town and he explained that the power in his neighborhood had gone out.

"So you overslept?" Bilderback probed, trying to get a rise out of the crowd.

"No," Benner replied, "my electric garage door wouldn't work, so I couldn't get my car out."

"So how did you get to school, Ben?"

"I did what I could," Benner said. "I ran."

Bilderback went slack-jawed.

I never got tired of hearing that story.

The sun was just beginning to break through the morning fog as Benner herded us to the starting line. Some runners mumbled prayers or made the sign of the cross on their chests. I just bit my lip.

I'd been too nervous to eat for the last twenty-four hours. Now I was feeling nauseated, and my muscles were tight. I had to get advice from Benner.

"Something's wrong with my legs!" I told him. "They don't feel normal. What should I do?"

"Go out there and run to the best of your ability," he replied. "Don't run with your legs. Run with your heart."

On some level, even as a high school freshman, I got his meaning: the human body has limitations; the human spirit is boundless. I didn't need a wristwatch to set the pace; I needed to run with my heart. I walked to the starting line focused and composed. The next few miles would influence the course of my life.

The gun fired and the race was on. Initially the course went straight on a well groomed and relatively wide grass path. My two strongest teammates, Fogerty and Fry, took an early lead. I settled into a secondary cluster of runners and tried to find a clearing among them. But the more I jockeyed for position, the more compressed the group became. The runners surrounded me; I had to break out of the pack or risk running at a tempo dictated by runners on the opposing team.

There is always tremendous risk involved in a "breakaway," especially at an early stage. It means temporarily pushing at an unsustainable level and hoping that the energy you expend won't prevent a strong finishing kick. It was a risk I had to take. I picked up my pace dramatically and pulled ahead of the majority of the pack, but two runners chased after me.

They began to draft off of me, hiding in my windshadow and using me as a blockade to cut the air. I didn't mind having one runner behind me, but two of them was too much. I kicked up my pace another notch and was able to drop one of them, but the other held tight. We came around a tree-lined bend in the course and encountered a brisk headwind, which made me feel the weight of the other runner, who stuck to my back like a lamprey, drafting so tightly I could feel his breath on the back of my neck. I slowed, tactically, hoping he would pass me so that I could draft off him for a while. But he was smarter than that. He slowed right down with me, staying behind me. And now, since I had reduced my speed, I could hear the pack we had just pulled away from catching up behind us.

The course dropped down a small embankment and narrowed. It was time to make another move. Just as the pack reached the back of the runner behind me, I turned on the afterburners. This time when I blasted out into the open, nobody followed me. I put my head down and plowed into the oncoming wind with all my might. The runner who had been behind me couldn't keep up, and now he had the entire pack drafting off him. It was beautiful!

Could I possibly sustain this margin for the rest of the race without blowing apart? With about a mile left in the course, I started to have doubts. My heart felt like it would pound right through my chest. My breathing was shallow and erratic, and every muscle in my body screamed in agony. I was forced to slow down to avoid blacking out, so I pulled back and plodded painfully along, waiting for the pack to rocket by me. I'd blown it; I'd pushed too hard too early in the race. Man, was this going to be humiliating.

But the pack didn't roar past me—apparently we had all gone out too hard. The path underfoot had become wet—clumps of grass and debris flying out from under my shoes—when suddenly the finish line appeared in the distance. If I could just hold on, this would be the best race of my life. I discovered a will to push harder than I'd ever gone before. I needed to hold my position; it meant the world to me. I couldn't let anybody pass.

In my peripheral vision, I could see three or four runners coming up quickly. They were now less than a pace behind me. Then two of them began to pass me, one on either side. Their arms were pumping and their necks craned to pull in front of me.

They pulled ahead by a step or two, blocking me out—a solid wall in front of me. Then another runner began passing me on the right. I glanced back to see four or five others right behind him. *Shit!* It was time to dig deeper, to give it everything I had, so I started sprinting at full speed.

Even then, I couldn't manage to break through that two-man wall running in front of me. I tried to pass on the right side, then the left, to no avail. The runners seemed to be working in unison to block me out.

The finish line was now 300 yards away. People on both sides of the course were yelling, "GO, KARNO, GO!" *To hell with their blockade,* I thought to myself. *If they won't let me pass, I'll run right through them.*

For a moment the two runners separated a notch, and I rammed myself between them. As I did, the guy on the right swung his left elbow high and caught me squarely on the bridge of my nose. The pain was a shock, but I wouldn't let it slow me down. I shook my head sharply, crammed my shoulders deeper into the gap, and forced my way through.

Grass and mud were flying everywhere and I could feel warm liquid pouring down my mouth, chin, and jersey— maybe sweat. Through the scattering debris, the banner above the finish line came into focus. In a mad dash, I pumped my arms wildly to try to pull ahead of my adversaries. The three of us burst across the line like battling racehorses.

I was hunched over with my hands on my knees, gasping for air, not knowing who'd won. That's when the dog-pile started. Someone jumped on my back, then another, and another. With my face pressed to the grass by the weight of at least six people, and someone's knee in my jaw, I heard one of them yell, "We won! We won!"

We had just become the champions of one of the toughest leagues in Southern California. I later learned that a handful of rival runners had finished within seconds of my time. If even one of them had been in front of me, we would have lost.

Struggling to my feet, I wiped my face and was shocked to see that the back of my hand was bright red. The blow I'd taken while busting through the two runners had resulted in a radical nosebleed; the entire front of my shirt was soaked with blood.

"Whoa," I said to Fogerty, holding out my jersey.

He chuckled. "Yeah, you ran the last hundred feet covered in blood. The crowd was going wild!"

When my team stepped up to the podium to accept our medals, it was one of the proudest moments of my life, rivaling the ten-hour bike ride to my grandparents' house a few years back. My head could be battered and bloodied, my muscles could ache for weeks, but nothing could replace the feelings of pride that came from physical accomplishment, feelings I carry to this day.

Coming home and sharing my medal with the family was glorious. They were so proud, and I felt as though I'd done my family right. Pary marveled at the colorful steel adornment but knew that it wasn't the medal that mattered; it was the sweat and blood that went into winning it that was the real prize. She looked at it, then she looked at me, and said, "This is so cool."

The season concluded with a celebratory banquet, at which I was awarded the "Most Inspirational" team member. I wasn't entirely sure how to interpret the award. "Most Inspirational" could mean that I'd displayed exemplary courage and determination. Or it could mean, "This crazy sonofabitch was willing to subject himself to more punishment than anyone else, so we had to give him something." I guess both were accurate.

Benner's retirement neared, and many of the team members drifted off. Occasionally I would run into some of the guys and we'd talk smack, but it just wasn't the same. Together, we'd shared an incredible moment, but life moves fast, especially in high school.

Later that year, I bumped into Benner one day at the beach. He was just coming in from the water. The shriveled skin on his hands and feet meant that he'd been out there a while, perhaps napping. I thanked him for the advice he'd given me before the league championships. Benner had instilled in me a passion for running, and his lessons on life were just as valuable. Running is about finding your inner peace, and so is a life well lived. "Run with your heart," he had told me.

I ran my first marathon later that year. It wasn't an organized race, but a fund-raiser for underprivileged children. We students collected pledges for each lap that was completed on the high school track. Donors typically pledged a dollar per mile, and most of my classmates ran between 2.5 and 4 miles—about 10 to 15 laps.

I ran 105. It took almost six hours to get through it, but I simply wouldn't stop until I'd completed the equivalent of a marathon. It was dark and deserted when I finished, except for a few die-hard friends who were blown away by my persistence.

You should have seen the look on people's faces when I told them they owed $105. Shock, mainly. A fair share of congratulatory gestures. And a few brow-raising disbelievers, who quickly paid up when I removed my shoe and showed them the blisters.

There had been a girl on the track during the run earlier in the day who had intrigued me. She was stunning, and even more so because she was covered in sweat. Most of the "beauty queens" at our school would have nothing to do with running or sweating in public. But she was a beauty who didn't seem to mind. I dug the way she looked, all flushed and exhausted, trying to complete another lap around the track.

I found out she was a freshman and that her name was Julie. Eventually I got up the courage to ask her to a movie. *Grease? Saturday Night Fever?* I can't remember. All I remember is her; that she was next to me, that she was on a date with me. I mean, the seniors and star jocks wanted to go out with her. Sure, I was an athlete, but an offbeat one. I didn't play baseball or football; I went running and surfed. I thought she belonged with the varsity quarterback, and there she was with me.

It was my first date ever, and I fell in love—not just some fleeting high school infatuation, but genuine, head-over-heels in love. Reflecting back, that is how I did things. Either a 100 percent commitment, total unwavering devotion, or nothing at all. Falling in love was no exception.

The two of us became inseparable. In keeping with Greek tradition, Julie became part of our family and didn't seem at all uncomfortable with the custom, even though she was a reserved WASP in a house full of boisterous Greeks. She seemed at ease during holiday gatherings filled with bantering relatives, flowing ouzo, broken plates, and living-room dancing.

Like my sister, Pary, Julie was the only girl in her family, and their friendship grew exceptionally strong. The two of them seemed to share a particular poise and composure, even in a room filled with domineering Greek men. Julie could hold her own against any ouzo-influenced chauvinistic uncle, in a spirited and fun way. Her quick wit won us all over, as she learned a couple of choice Greek words and would humorously spring them on unsuspecting assailants at the most opportune times.

Now that the cross-country season was over, there was only one organized option to keep me running—join the track team. Track season began after cross-country season ended. It was almost like defecting to the enemy, but I let my love of running get the better of me.

Bilderback, the track coach, put me on the team without a formal tryout, which was nice enough. But my first encounter with him as a coach was disastrous. I showed up for practice on the first day and, as usual, wasn't wearing a watch. He had me run a series of time-trials. As I completed each lap, he looked at his stopwatch and yelled out the times, banging on a clipboard with his pen as he screamed.

This was irritating. I'd done well in cross-country without someone barking orders every time I ran. So after Bilderback had clocked me, measured me, evaluated my stride, and dissected my split times, I mentioned that there was really no need to scream out my times as I ran.

"But if you don't know what your split times are," he said, "how do you pace yourself?"

"I run with my heart," I replied.

That was about the funniest damn thing Bilderback had ever heard. "He runs with his heart!" he whooped between gales of laughter. "He runs with his heart!"

I wanted to punch the bastard. Instead, I walked off the track and hung up my shoes.

I didn't run again for fifteen years.

Chapter 4

Run for Your Life

Not life, but good life, is to be chiefly valued.

—Socrates

Southern to Northern California
1977–1992

My running career ended, but life carried on without much remorse. With three high school kids in the house, there was no shortage of revelry. After running, things got unruly. I discovered alcohol and began throwing underage parties when the folks were away. Kraig and I started battling. He hocked my motorcycle to buy a new surfboard, and we got into a brawl in the living room over it, breaking china and putting a big hole in the wall. It was typically me or my brother who caused most of the ruckus, and I was clearly the worst offender, like the time I commandeered the family car and drove to Mexico without a license. Pary was always the stable one.

Growing up the only girl in a Greek family was not easy. Our father was overprotective and rarely allowed her to stray far from home. It was especially hard for him because Pary was quite beautiful—long golden hair, deep brown eyes, olive skin, and a Julia Roberts smile. My poor father constantly worried about her safety, and about boys. Pary was unruffled by it, though, and never rebelled. She was comfortable with herself, and lots of people, like me, were drawn to her inner strength.

Pary and I remained the best of friends throughout high school. She was my closest confidante and never judged me, no matter how far I deviated from her values or how badly I screwed up. And boy, did I ever screw up badly, being expelled twice for showing up to school functions intoxicated. My parents were livid, ready to ship me off to boarding school, but Pary stuck by my side, as if she knew this unsettled phase of mine would pass. I admired her whimsical way of always moving forward, never taking life too seriously. "They still love you," she said, speaking about my parents —"just give it some time." We were family, and even in the worst of circumstances, we had each other. That's what mattered.

High school graduation came and passed, and I headed off to college at Cal Poly, where the debauchery continued, only without adult supervision to get in the way. I was miles from home and carefree, not to mention careless. With a newly acquired fake ID, booze was easy to come by, and every night seemed cause for celebration. I surfed and windsurfed all day, occasionally attending class when time permitted, and then partied into the wee hours. My energy needed an outlet, and all-night binges filled that need.

Julie and I remained together, but I could sense she was tiring of my ways. She had decided to attend Baylor University in Texas, and we vowed to keep our relationship alive, though I had doubts she would remain loyal, given the way I was behaving. And who could blame her?

Then, early one morning, after a particularly wild evening, someone knocked on my apartment door. It was a priest. The night before, Pary had lost control of the convertible she was driving; she was thrown from the vehicle as it rolled, and killed. It was the eve of her eighteenth birthday.

The blow to my family went beyond shock and sadness. One day she was a healthy and vibrant young lady, and the next she was gone. Her sudden disappearance opened a chasm of despair among us. The void it left in my own life was unbearable.

The rift her death created in our family seemed bottomless. A part of us was missing, irreplaceable, gone forever. We had suffered through low points as a family in the past, but we had always maintained a certain optimism that the situation would change, things would get better. At the very least, we always had one another. Until now.

My kid sister, Pary

She was gone, and our family was destroyed. Gatherings were no longer a time of celebration, but of mourning. As the years passed, I tried to restore some sense of joy to our household. I cleaned up my act and started spending weekends back home. Kraig and I settled our sibling differences and became close friends. We adopted a new pet for our parents, a playful Golden Lab puppy. But nothing could console them.

After years of trying, I finally gave up.

A few years after my sister's death, my dad started doing something curious. He started running. More precisely, he started training for the Los Angeles Marathon. He would run during his lunch break, after getting home from work, and early in the morning. He stuck to his routine with extraordinary conviction and gradually prepared himself for the challenge.

When the gun went off, he was ready. The race hurt him bad, but he kept going. Wouldn't stop until crossing the finish line, despite the pain. Though it was unspoken, I think it was his way of paying tribute to my sister. As they carried him into the medical tent, swollen and cramping, he was smiling defiantly.

From that day forward, no matter that he ran less after completing the event, I always thought of my dad, foremost, as a marathoner. Which, to me, was the greatest distinction there could be.

Eventually I graduated from college, more by dint of grit and sweat than of scholarship. After losing my sister, I couldn't bring myself to saddle my parents with the financial obligation of putting me through school. It just didn't seem right. So I paid for most of my education by hustling for scholarships and grants and working at the campus health-care center. I wasn't the smartest kid in school, but few had more drive or worked harder. Partying was now the last thing on my mind.

Even though I hadn't run in years, outdoor sports remained important to me. I did some mountain climbing and scuba diving, but I channeled most of my focus into windsurfing, winning some competitions and ending up on the cover of several magazines. I even managed to land a few sponsorship endorsements, which helped pay the tuition bills.

When graduation rolled around, I was somewhat amazed to learn that I was the class valedictorian. When the dean first informed me, I thought it was a commencement prank. Clearly the honor belonged to one of my brainy classmates. My marks had been good, sure, but entirely on account of the extra effort I put into my studies. Academics didn't come easy to me; I had to work doubly hard just to keep up. But it was true, I had finished at the top of my class.

After my undergraduate degree came graduate school at Cal Poly San Luis Obispo. And after graduate school came business school at USF's McLaren School of Business and Management. I now took school more seriously, which surprised even me. I was more interested in climbing corporate ladders than mountains.

Julie and I remained together through college. After Pary's death, our commitment to each other strengthened, and there was no breaking the bond. She moved back to California upon completing her degree, and we got married shortly thereafter. We settled happily in the city we loved, San Francisco, and life was cozy. I began rising up the ranks in the marketing department of a major health-care company, making decent money and living the idyllic yuppie lifestyle.

The past slowly melted away. I tried not to think about anything beyond the immediate. For the moment, I was content—at least as far as I could tell.

As the years rolled by, however, the job pressures began to mount, and the car payments and hefty mortgage didn't help. Suddenly, work was stressing me out. The long hours and the travel were becoming mundane. At first it was glamorous, but somewhere among all the meetings, dinners, and cocktail receptions, I became aware of an inner hollowness. Something was missing in my life.

Work wasn't providing the satisfaction that I had always thought it would. So what if I had an MBA and was pulling in six figures a year? There was an emptiness that my career didn't fulfill. I began to secretly long to fill this void, even though I wasn't sure what it was or how it could be filled.

One day, as my thirtieth birthday approached, a call at my desk shook me from one of my increasingly frequent daydreams.

"Dean, Dr. Naish here." Naish was the CEO of a large potential client that I'd been pitching for months. "The board has had the opportunity to deliberate, and I am happy to inform you that you've been awarded the contract."

I silently pumped my fist in the air.

"We're looking forward to doing business with you folks," Naish continued. "I'll have my admin set up a meeting for later this week."

"*Right on!*" I shouted when we'd hung up. This was a contract my company wanted badly. The news would be celebrated. I called my boss to give him the good word.

"*Yes!*" he yelled into the receiver. I could hear him punching numbers into his calculator. "You know how big your commission check is going to be?!"

With a sudden sense of deflation, I realized that I didn't care. My check might be big, but it seemed that the toll the job was taking on me was even bigger. Every day I'd field dozens of urgent voicemail messages and dozens more e-mails. Managing all of that incoming noise was nearly impossible. At some point the clamor had begun to manage me. Now I just reacted to the events of the day, not setting my own course in any substantive way, not feeling any real sense of accomplishment. At first the money mattered, because I had never had any. But now that I'd managed to accumulate a modest stockpile, I realized there had to be more to life than continually trying to bolster those reserves.

For the better part of my adult life I'd been making deadlines and chasing the next deal. It had been so long since I had stopped to reflect, I wasn't sure what was important any longer. Things were moving so fast that there was no time to look below the surface. Everyone around me seemed to be operating on the same level, and it just fed on itself. We were all caught up in a whirlwind of important meetings and expensive lunches, do-or-die negotiations, lucrative deals conducted in fancy hotels with warmed towel racks and monogrammed robes.

I had grown accustomed to the upscale lifestyle, the bonuses, the hefty options package. My future looked bright as the perks continued to roll in. But I couldn't ignore the nagging sense that something was missing. I was moving fast, that was for sure, but was I moving forward? I needed a sense of purpose and clarity—and, perhaps, *adventure.*

Something snapped on the morning of my thirtieth birthday. It began pleasantly with Julie bringing me breakfast in bed.

"Happy birthday, darling," she smiled, pouring my coffee. "Can you believe you're thirty years old?"

That simple question, which slid so innocently from her mouth, sent me into an absolute tailspin. For the first time it hit me—*I was thirty years old!* How could it be?

I felt as though I hadn't even begun to live yet. How could I be thirty? Where had the years gone?

At that moment I realized that my life was being wasted. Disillusioned with the trappings of the corporate scene, the things that really mattered—friendship and exploration, personal expansion and a sense of meaning—had gotten all twisted around making a lot of money and buying stuff. I hungered for a place where I could explore nature and my capabilities, away from a corporate office in a corporate building in a big city with crowded supermalls and people judging me by the car I drove (which, of course, was a new Lexus).

What I needed was some breathing room to figure things out. Some space to determine what really mattered to me. I needed a chance to clear my vision and look at the world through fresh eyes.

"Honey, is everything all right?" Julie asked. "You look like you're a mile away."

"No, it's not," I replied. "I'm confused. I feel trapped by my routine of twelve-hour workdays. I'm not sure what's important anymore. My fear is that I'll wake up thirty years from now and be in the same place, only wrinkled and bald . . . and really fat. And bitter."

"Wow," she said. "Is the coffee too strong?"

"I read a story in the paper yesterday about the first mountain climber to scale Mount Everest without supplemental oxygen," I said. "Nobody thought it was remotely possible to climb the highest mountain in the

Run for Your Life 51

world without using bottled oxygen, but this guy went and did it anyway. A reporter asked him afterward why he had gone up there to die, and you know how he responded? 'I didn't go up there to die, I went up there to live.' "

She listened politely, but I could see my ramblings weren't entirely clear.

"I miss my sister," I said, "and the good times we used to have together. I want my family to come back together. I'm sick of work being the center of my life, it's just not doing it for me. Something's missing. Is thirty too young to be having a midlife crisis?"

We spent the rest of the day kicking around the city, not saying much. I picked at my food when we stopped for lunch at an outdoor cafe.

That evening we joined friends for drinks at the Paragon, a swanky nightclub in San Francisco's hip Marina District. The city was hopping, all the trendy bars mobbed with self-important young professionals like myself. Julie, who isn't big on nightlife, decided to walk home early. I stayed out with the boys and proceeded to get seriously loaded for the first time in years. At one point a beautiful young woman said hello to one of my friends, and he introduced her to me.

"This is Dean. It's his thirtieth birthday."

It was an embarrassing statement, and I hoped that she would ignore it. But she didn't.

"Well, hello, Dean," she said, squeezing my hand most pleasantly. "How's it feel to be thirty?"

Extremely troubling, I thought. But I blurted "Great!" with a phony, drunken grin on my face.

She lived in San Francisco, too, and worked downtown. She told me that she rarely went to bars, which I doubted. I bought her a drink. And then she bought me a drink. We toasted my birthday. In the back of my mind, the part that was still sober, I could see where things might be heading, and I really didn't want to go there.

Then again, I was drunk. And depressed. And this girl was really cute. The bar was pulsing to a jazz band, and we swayed along, chatting away. Soon enough, she was rubbing against me, her face lit up by a seductive smile.

"I have a confession to make," I managed to say. "I'm married."

"I know," she smiled. "I saw your ring. So am I."

She held up her left hand to display a massive rock on her finger.

"So, can I buy you another drink, birthday boy?" She pressed herself against me again.

My mind was whirling. "Hold that thought," I said. "Let me run to the restroom."

As I worked my way through the crowd, my heart began to speak. When I reached the restroom, I didn't stop. I kept going, into the kitchen, where, behind the gas stoves and walk-in coolers, there was a delivery entrance. I pushed my way out through this door into the tradesmen's alley, then made my way among the food remains and rubbish to the street.

And kept walking.

The cool night air cleared my head almost immediately. The streets of San Francisco were quiet, except for the foghorn on the Golden Gate Bridge, reverberating off in the distance. Light trails of mist swept down the streets, and the moon appeared, and then disappeared, behind the clouds. It was late and dark, and very still once I got out of that bar.

When I reached my house a few blocks from the bar, I saw that Julie had left the porch light on. Our Victorian looked warm and inviting, and safe. I began walking up the stairs, like I'd done a thousand times before, but I only made it a few steps.

There was something transforming about tonight. A switch had been flipped inside me. I wasn't going to check my messages and then slip into the comfort of my warm bed. There was a determination to make tomorrow morning different, too. I wouldn't be showing up at the office as usual, only to exchange gripes with my colleagues about how our jobs had taken over our lives and how there was no time left for anything else.

I'd no longer stand for it. This was my life, and I was damn well going to live it on my terms. Over the years I'd softened, lost my edge. But that was all about to change tonight.

I went to the garage and cautiously made my way through the darkness to the back porch, where I kept an old pair of sneakers used for yard work. I deliberated for a moment about what else to wear. After some thought, I undid my belt and pulled off my pants. I had on a pair of loose-fitting jockey briefs, which would be comfortable enough. I took off my sweater but left my undershirt on. The socks were a problem. They were black silk knee-highs. I folded them down low around my ankles, then put on the sneakers.

In my pants pocket I found a twenty-dollar bill. It had started the evening as a hundred-dollar bill, but the bar had consumed the balance. Folding it up neatly and stuffing it into my shoe, I took a swig of water from the hose, and made my way back to the street.

As I started jogging south, I turned to take one last look at my house. Inside was my beautiful wife, peacefully asleep. I blew her a kiss and strode out of sight.

It was tough going. I hadn't run any real distance in fifteen years. But I kept at it. That night I just *knew* I had to keep at it.

So I ran, and became filled with emotions and memories. I thought about my sister, Pary, and how much I missed her every day, even now, almost a decade after her passing. I thought about the time I had teased her about not liking ketchup, and wished that I hadn't. And I thought about the time Pary, Julie, and I had ditched school and driven to Disneyland, eaten cotton candy and gone on all the rides, joked with Mickey—because he knew we were playing hooky and didn't mind—and held hands and skipped through Tomorrowland, singing, *"Yo ho, yo ho, a pirate's life for me!"* and then snuck Julie back into her house afterward. Was I ever grateful for that day.

These memories carried me along pleasantly as I ran.

Three hours later, exhaustion set in. And hunger. Steady running requires an almost steady supply of fuel. My stomach felt like a deflated balloon. Happily, I saw the lights of a Taco Bell up ahead. My stomach growled and twisted itself into knots of anticipation as I staggered up to the front door. The sign clearly said OPEN LATE, but the door was locked. Bummer. I was sunk.

I sat down on the curb to catch my breath. My feet were swollen, and my left big toe was aching terribly. I pulled off that shoe. What I found was appalling. The front of my sock was discolored and soaked with pus. When I got it off, I saw the massive blood blister that had popped on the tip of the toe and had caused the stain.

Great. I'd covered only fifteen miles and already I was maimed. I should have known that my gardening sneakers weren't suitable for long-distance running. But I hadn't owned running shoes in quite some time, hadn't had much occasion to use them.

I was staring at this bloody mess when I heard a car pull around from behind the building and saw that food was being served through the drive-up window. Yes, they were open! I was saved!

My legs throbbing and cramped, my foot mangled, my body coated in a layer of sweat and road grime, I hobbled around back to the drive-through speaker. I stomped on the cord with my heel. "Can I take your order?" a tinny voice asked.

"Oh, yes!" I cried. "To start, I'll have two tacos, a burrito supreme, and two tostadas."

"Will that be it?"

"And a large Coke and two bean burritos."

"Anything more?"

"That'll do it."

"Please pay at the window."

Digging the crumpled twenty out of my shoe, I strolled joyously to the pick-up window. The girl up there didn't look so happy, however.

"Sir, do you have a vehicle? You cannot order food from the drive-through unless you're in a car."

I studied her. She was just a kid. No doubt the manager had drilled this rule into her. And I couldn't have been a reassuring sight. But she was standing up there between me and my tacos. This was going to require some of the delicate persuasion skills I'd acquired at work. I tried my most winning smile.

"I understand what you're saying," I said, calmly and agreeably. "But in this one isolated instance, could you just let it slide? I won't do it again, promise."

She peered down at me, my sagging underpants fraying and tattered.

"Nice try."

"Look, I've got the money right here, and I can see my order right there." I was still smiling, and trying to keep the note of hysteria out of my voice. "Let's just make a quick transaction and we'll be done with it. No one will ever know."

"I'm sorry, sir, but if we make an exception for you, we'd have to let everyone order from the drive-through without a car."

What was she talking about? I wondered. I looked behind me. Not a single other thirty-year-old man in his underpants appeared to be trying to sneak through the Taco Bell drive-through in the middle of the night.

I showed her the twenty again.

"Please. Let me have my order and you can keep the change."

"Good night, sir."

"But . . ."

She disappeared from the window.

"Food!" I moaned. "I need food!"

Just then a car approached the drive-through, a massive, late-model Oldsmobile. I hobbled over as the middle-aged Asian driver rolled down his window. He looked surprised but not frightened to see me, which was a good sign.

"Listen, I'm really hungry," I told him softly, so as not to be overheard by Helga the Taco Nazi inside. "They won't let me order. I need to go in your car through this drive-up window."

"Where your car?" he asked.

"My car is in San Francisco."

"You want a ride to San Francisco?"

"No. I just go with you through this drive-through to get food." He looked like a tough negotiator. "If you drive me through, I'll pay for your food."

That cracked him up. "You pay? You crazy! You crazy, man."

Still laughing, he waved me around to the passenger side. I didn't want Helga to see me next to him, so I slipped into the backseat and hunkered there, hopefully out of sight.

"We play taxi?" he grinned. "Okay, I taxi man. What you order?"

"Order me eight tacos," I said softly.

"Eight tacos!" he cried. I motioned for him to keep it down.

Helga seemed very suspicious through her whole exchange with him, but he pulled it off beautifully. There was a touchy moment at the window when I passed him my crumpled twenty and he held it up to her. She furrowed her eyebrows at it, and I could see she was wondering if and where she'd last seen it. I held my breath. Finally, with measured reluctance, she took the money and handed over the blessed sacks of treats.

My driver was giggling delightedly as we pulled away. "You so crazy!" he kept saying. He pulled the car into a nearby parking lot and cut the engine. "We eat now?"

Who was this guy? I wondered. How many nights had he eaten Mexican food alone in this empty parking lot? Did he have anywhere to go? Why was he so willing to pick up a stranger?

But it was time for me to move on, and these questions would remain unanswered. "I can't stay," I told him as I got out. I came around to his window and he handed me my bag of tacos.

"You crazy," he grinned. "How much I owe you?"

"Nothing," I smiled back. "And you the crazy one. Thanks."

We shook hands and I started moving up the road, unwrapping a taco as I jogged off into the distance. It was tricky trying to eat while running. At one point I accidentally inhaled while chewing and sucked a piece of diced tomato into the back of my throat. For a moment I thought I would choke on it, but what surfaced instead was a sneeze. And with that sneeze came the chunk of tomato shooting out my nostril. A hardy layer of sour cream helped lubricate its passage, and it deposited a foul, acidic slime in my nasal canal upon exiting.

My wounded toe was killing me. It's funny how the pain would come and go in waves. At times the throbbing was so excruciating I could hardly put any weight on it. Yet during the lulls it was almost imperceptible. Eventually the entire front of my foot went numb.

As I ran farther south along the San Francisco peninsula, the urban landscape slowly gave way to rolling coastal foothills. Traversing a ridge to the west of the bay, I saw the colored runway lights of SFO flickering off in the distance. Low over the horizon, the sparkling headlights of incoming planes were stacked in the sky. I crested the coastal ridge and began dropping down the west side of the divide toward the ocean. The lights of Silicon Valley were no longer visible, and it grew progressively darker. Although the area was mostly undeveloped, periodically I would pass small rows of houses that lined the silent back road. Occasionally there would be a light on inside, or the translucent blue glow of a TV set, but mostly the houses were dark, which was probably for the best. Imagine walking out of your house at 4:00 A.M. to see a man in his underwear running by, struggling as though each step were his last. "Asylum escapee" would be my first thought.

The night air turned misty and damp the farther west I ran toward the coastline. Puddles formed along the road from condensation dripping off the trees above, and the pungent scents of pine and eucalyptus drifted in the air. A skunk meandered out of the bushes. He turned to look at me but didn't seem particularly concerned by my presence. I, on the other hand, was more than a bit concerned by his. Luckily, our encounter was stench-free.

After running up and down several peaks and valleys, I made my way down into one markedly deeper trough. It was cold and foggy in the pit of this gorge, and the climb up the other side was brutally steep. It seemed to go on forever. Just when the road appeared to be leveling off, there would be yet another uphill section. The fog was thick. After doing battle with this beast of a hill for as long as I could, it got the better of me. I stopped to regroup, and stood hunched over and panting on the side of the road, wondering how much more abuse my body could possibly take.

After a brief reprieve, I lifted my head to notice slight breaks in the clouds. I'd nearly climbed above the fog line. I was conquering that hill, nearing the top, and I hadn't even noticed it. Something about this realization lifted my spirits. Things were becoming clearer. I put my head down, ignored the pain, and started back up the rise at a brisk pace—which, after running twenty-five miles, was about the equivalent of a moderate walk.

Though my legs screamed for mercy, each step brought a brighter view of the sky above, and the air seemed warmer and drier the higher I climbed. Perspiration poured down my face, despite the cool fog surrounding me. Then, as though I had abruptly punched through a breaking wave, I found myself standing on top of the clouds. The sky was filled with stars that seemed to shine brighter than I had ever seen before. I felt I could reach up and grab a handful of sky. I was mesmerized by the stillness and the silence, totally absorbed in the moment.

For the first time this evening—hell, for the first time in years—I felt like this spot was precisely where I belonged . . . never mind that I was half naked, in the middle of nowhere, and nearly incapable of taking another step forward. That was inconsequential. I was happy— entirely content just standing there. I had listened to my heart, and this is where it had led me.

The sun was coming up when I reached the town of Half Moon Bay along the San Mateo coast. I had run for seven hours straight through the night and covered thirty miles. I'd long since passed through delirium and was now in a semi-catatonic state. Events seemed to unfold in front of me as though I were watching a motion picture. In other words, I needed coffee. Badly.

Many of the inhabitants of Half Moon Bay commute "over the hill" into Silicon Valley, which they were now beginning to do in a frenzy of traffic. It was as if someone had switched the projector to fast forward, and all the commuter ants were busily scurrying around in hyperdrive.

I found a pay phone and placed a collect call to home, waking Julie.

"Where are you?"

"It's a long story. The short version is that I'm out in front of a 7-Eleven."

"Seven-Eleven on Geary Street?"

"No, 7-Eleven in Half Moon Bay," I said hoarsely. "Can you come get me?"

"Half Moon Bay?! How did you get down there?"

"I ran."

"You what? You ran? From where?"

"From the house. I got here about five minutes ago."

"You mean you ran all night?" she said in shock. "My God, are you okay?"

"I think so. I've lost control of my leg muscles, and my feet are swollen stuck in my shoes. I'm standing here in my underwear. But other than that, I'm doing pretty well. Actually, I feel strangely alive."

I could hear her moving around the room, gathering her things. "You don't sound too stable. Just hold tight and I'll get down there as soon as I can. Is there anything I can bring you? Food? Clothing?"

"Yeah," I said nonchalantly, trying not to alarm her. "Please grab our insurance card. I might need to stop by the hospital on the way home."

When Julie found me she was stunned, and delighted. She wanted to know all about my adventure, and I was eager to tell her the story, except that I passed out in the car scarcely a minute into the drive home. The last thing I remember was a string of drool dangling off my yapping chin as Julie gazed over at me in bewilderment. Then things went black.

And that's how I became a runner once again. In the course of a single night I had been transformed from a drunken yuppie fool into a reborn athlete. During a period of great emptiness in my life, I turned to running for strength. I heard the calling, and I went to the light.

For weeks after my thirty-mile jaunt I was nearly incapacitated from muscle spasms and inflammation. But it was a good hurt, one that would make Coach McTavish proud. As I limped around my office, trying to appear natural, I reminded myself that pain and suffering are often the catalysts for life's most profound lessons. A passion I'd ignored for half my existence had been serendipitously reignited in one all-night thirty-mile hullabaloo. The resulting ice packs and tubes of Ben-Gay were a small price to pay.

Every devout runner has an awakening. We know the place, the time, and the reason we accepted running into our life. After half a lifetime, I'd been reborn. Most runners are able to keep a rational perspective on the devotion, and practice responsibly. I couldn't, and became a fanatic.

Chapter 5

The Soiling of the Lexus

No guts, no glory.

—World War II slogan

San Francisco
1992–1993

It took weeks to recuperate from my thirty-mile reawakening. The blisters on my toes eventually healed, the muscle soreness subsided, the shin splints eased. I felt enough joy from the experience to keep the running going. Four nights a week, right after work, I would change into my new jogging gear and hit the road. I started with just a few miles per outing, but I soon increased that to five or six miles a day. Like most runners, I had favorite routes that I'd clocked with my car, noting the mile markers along the way.

I'd frequently see the same fellow runners on my route: the guy being pulled along by his black Labrador, the older couple who always ran together, the tough-looking kid with the awkward gait. We'd exchange pleasantries. Near the beginning of the run, it could be an energized wave accompanied by actual verbal communication, like "Hi." Toward the end of an outing, it would be little more than a nod—even an eyebrow lift was a stretch on the really tough days.

Focusing on work in the afternoon became increasingly difficult because I couldn't wait to head off for a run. Julie would watch with amusement as I dashed in through the door and threw on my running gear. We'd briefly trade small talk, and I'd always depart with a hug and a peck on the cheek, but she could sense that my mind was somewhere else. She was supportive of my running from the onset, largely because my mood was always upbeat afterward. Although we spent less time together, it was a more meaningful connection when we did. I was less distracted, having worked through the issues of the day on the run, my mind uncluttered and available.

As my level of fitness improved, I'd cover the same distance in fewer minutes. Sometimes I'd even get spirited and sprint the last hundred yards. I was really proud about my level of endurance, as if I'd reached some imaginary pinnacle on the fitness stud-o-meter. But one warm fall evening, my delusions were shattered.

It happened as I was finishing a run along the San

Francisco waterfront, thinking about how markedly my stamina had improved since I'd taken up running again. The final stretch of the run involved a climb through the Presidio military base along a particularly steep path known as Lovers' Lane. The name dates back to the late 1800s, when enlisted men used to walk from the Presidio to the Mission District in search of a good time. They would leave the base along this steep path and, if lucky, would have a female companion accompanying them on the walk back.

I was cruising up Lovers' Lane at a pretty good clip, feeling good about my pace and stamina. Suddenly, two men in military fatigues and backpacks blew right past me. They disappeared up the hill in a cloud of dust.

Wow, I thought. How were they able to pass me with such gusto? They'll probably stop and rest at the top, and I'll pass them. They're probably just running wind sprints. There's no way they could hold that pace for long, especially with those packs on their backs.

Not a minute later, though, the two men came charging back down. My running cap nearly flew off as they roared past me, and I coughed feebly on the dust cloud they kicked up.

What happened next was astounding. Just as I was getting ready to crest the summit of the hill, the pair came blasting up behind me again! Were they going to lap me once more, or would they rest at the top this time? They did neither. Instead, they dropped to the ground and started doing push-ups. And, as if to rub it in my face, they kept their packs on.

This was too much. These guys were playing in an entirely different league. No, a different *reality.* I walked over to them and said hello, but they just kept doing their push-ups.

"You guys training for something?" I asked.

After a long moment, the one on the left simply grunted, "Yeah."

I tried again. "It must be a pretty tough race, the way you guys are training. Are there hills involved?"

"No," the other one said. "There are mountains involved."

Not a talkative pair, but I was intrigued. "Is it some sort of race, or is it military training?"

"Race," came the reply.

There were a few more moments of silence. Then they simultaneously muttered "Fifty" and popped to their feet. The one on the right turned to me, raised both eyebrows, and said, "It's called the Western States One Hundred." And off they went back down the hill.

As I continued my run, I found it difficult to focus on anything except my physical inadequacy. My feelings of accomplishment and well-being were gone. In their place was one obsessive thought: *Just what is this Western States Endurance Run?*

Half an hour later, I walked through the door of my house, a man on a mission. As I showered and prepared for dinner, my mind was secretly plotting a way to sneak some personal research time into a typical workday filled with appointments and meetings.

During lunch the next day, I went to the library and found a few articles about the Western States 100-Mile Endurance Run. It was a continuous nonstop wilderness trek through the mountains and canyons of the Sierra Nevada range in California, where the peaks tower into the sky. Participants attempt to cover a 100-mile trail in under twenty-four hours, on foot.

Unbelievable. It didn't seem humanly possible to run 100 miles nonstop, let alone 100 miles through the mountains. That's nearly four marathons without rest, more than three times the distance that had left me temporarily incapacitated on my thirtieth birthday. No way could I possibly see myself attempting such an unimaginable feat.

But then I thought of those two runners blowing past me on Lovers' Lane. Somewhere in the soil of my mind, a seed took root.

The Western States 100-Mile Endurance Run didn't start as a run at all; its inception can be traced to a long-distance horse race, the Tevis Cup, 100 miles through the mountains on horseback. But in 1974, a man named Gordy Ainsleigh changed everything. Gordy had trained relentlessly with his horse for a year, and, as legend has it, just prior to the event his horse came up lame.

Crushed, but undeterred, Gordy announced that he

would still be competing in the 100-mile race, only without his horse.

This did more than raise a few eyebrows. It was complete lunacy. But on August 3, 1974, a bare-chested Gordy Ainsleigh took his place at the starting line of the Tevis Cup alongside a row of horses. Apparently right before the race began, one of his friends was overheard asking him whether he wanted a ham sandwich or a feed bag. Another bystander purportedly asked a race official if the event was reserved exclusively for animals. To which the official replied, "He *is* an animal."

Amazingly, twenty-three hours and forty-two minutes later, out from the trailhead popped Gordy. He was somewhat incoherent and despondent, but still shuffling forward. With a will of iron, he'd covered the entire 100 miles on foot. He even managed to beat a few of the horses.

It was this astonishing accomplishment that ushered in the modern era of ultra-endurance trail running.

Endurance is a relative term. Some might think a marathon, at 26.2 miles, with its two to five hours of continuous pounding to the body, is the ultimate test of human endurance. Hills make the undertaking all the more demanding; the Boston Marathon, for example, includes the infamous "Heartbreak Hill," a climb of 280 vertical feet. That's nearly the length of a football field straight up into the air. It's the vertical equivalent of climbing one quarter of the way to the top of the Empire State Building. Heartbreak Hill can be a demoralizing obstacle that forces many runners into submission, and they walk.

For an ultra-elite group of athletes, however, a single marathon is child's play. The challenges these individuals seek are beyond comprehension, bordering on psychotic. They participate in endeavors so physically demanding that some have perished in the act.

Near the top of the intensity scale is the Western States 100-Mile Endurance Run. It involves a total elevation change of 38,000 feet, climbing the equivalent of over fifty football fields straight up into the air. That would be like climbing the entire distance to the top of the Empire State Building and back down again—fifteen times! It means climbing and descending Heartbreak Hill not once, not twice, but fifty-six times. For a comparison of the Western States 100-Mile Endurance Run and the Boston Marathon, check out the chart below.

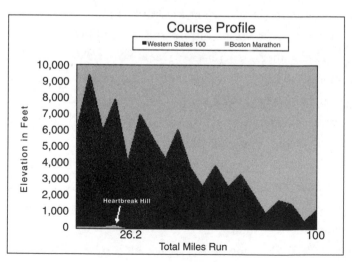

The Western States is run on rugged single-track mountain trails with harrowing drop-offs and unpredictable terrain. It crosses snow and ice fields, descends into murderously hot valleys, fords numerous bridgeless rivers, and offers little in the way of food, water, or medical support along the way. Of those who successfully complete the event—and sometimes fewer than half of the invited athletes do—it typically means twenty-five to thirty hours of continuous running.

Outside magazine once called the Western States the "toughest endurance event in the world." To complete it, your mental resolve must be indomitable. You've got to bundle up self-doubt and fear and stuff them in your shoe, cutting loose your rational mind as your body is pushed to inconceivable levels of endurance. To complete the Western States, you must transform yourself into a human machine.

My 5-mile jaunts around the city were sufficiently demanding in their own right. How would it be possible to extend that twenty times—through the mountains? Running thirty miles had debilitated me for weeks; attempting 100 might leave me dead. Sitting at my desk, in my tailored suit and leather loafers, thumbing through *Outside* with its photographs of sweating, struggling, brutalized, and barely coherent runners, I had just one thought:

Where do I sign up?

From that point forward, my life became passionately focused on gaining entrance into the Western States 100-Mile Endurance Run. Training became life; the rest was just details. Julie, who'd wanted to be a dentist since age six (when she got her first set of braces), had entered the University of the Pacific Dental School in San Francisco. This was an endurance event in its own right, and she was consumed with her studies. So there was balance, her studying into the wee hours and me running into the same. We had no children yet, so there was complete devotion to our personal goals.

To qualify for the Western States, you must complete a fifty-mile race in less than nine hours. Like the Boston Marathon, the Western States only accepts the elite. With the enthusiasm of a new recruit, I began a formal training program. I increased my four-days-a-week five-mile runs to six-days-a-week ten-mile runs, putting in the miles regardless of the weather or lack of motivation. No more junk food and soft drinks for me; I cut out saturated fat and all refined sugar from my diet, and read ingredient and nutritional facts on food labels with painstaking scrutiny. My typical lunch consisted of a piece of salmon with fresh vegetables. What I really missed at first were sweets. I craved candy and ice cream. But I began feeling so much better after eliminating sugars from my diet that eventually I hardly missed them.

After half a year of rigorous preparation, I found

myself capable of running a full marathon on any given day. And I was strong on the hills, San Francisco providing ample training grounds. Sometimes I would run a marathon on Saturday, before breakfast, and then another marathon on Sunday. One of my favorite routes took me up the Hyde Street hill, where I'd often race the cable cars to the cheers and jeers of the passengers. My legs grew powerful and my body became taut and lean.

Training so intensely required sacrifices in other areas of my life. A good athlete might be able to fake his way through a 10K, or perhaps even a marathon, but there's no running fifty miles without having paid your dues. I would get up well before dawn to run before work. Anywhere I traveled, either for work or pleasure, my running shoes came along. If there was a break in my day, even for forty-five minutes, I was out the door for a "quick pop," followed by a speedy sponge bath in the men's room, and then back into my suit for the next meeting.

I loved running, especially across the Golden Gate Bridge into the hills of Marin. Though some of my friends thought my antics were becoming a little overzealous, I hardly noticed that I'd progressed from a casual jogger into something more. Distances that I'd previously thought impossible were now covered without much notice. The good folks at the Fleet Feet running store kept my credit-card information on file, since I was in every few weeks to purchase new running shoes.

After months of preparation, I felt ready to take on the fifty-miler. The qualifying run was on a course set in the foothills of the Sierra Nevada, just outside Sacramento. It started at 5:00 A.M. and was a couple hours' drive from San Francisco, so I left my house at two in the morning.

The drive was luxurious. As a perk for my job performance, the company had given me a new Lexus LS 400 luxury sedan. I'm not much of a car guy, but it sure was a nice ride. The one thing that really struck me was how quiet it was inside. The seals on the doors were so efficient that the interior seemed almost soundproof.

When I got to the race, I was startled to discover that it was near-freezing outside—twenty degrees cooler than when I'd left the house. I sat in my new Lexus, with its heated leather seats, until just before the start.

Coincidentally, among the few dozen runners milling about the starting line were the pair who'd passed me on Lovers' Lane. I said hello. One of them raised his eyebrows at me, while the other didn't acknowledge my presence at all. Ah, such gentlemen. We all jammed into the small starting area, and with a few yelps and hoots the race began.

Within 3 miles of the start, I found myself running alone. There were only about forty racers, and the pack thinned quickly. The course meandered through the countryside, fairly flat and well groomed, with some sparse vegetation lining the trail. Periodically I would spot other runners ahead of me and behind me, but a reasonable distance separated the fleet. Aside from the aid stations along the route, I ran solo for the entire race.

It was a journey into uncharted waters, and I had no

one to consult for directions. So I did as Benner had instructed years ago, and ran with my heart. It was all that I knew to do.

There was only modest elevation change as we followed the well-traveled dirt path. As the race wore on, however, a freezing wind developed, and the path became a little less orderly. It was all very exciting to me. Even though I ran alone, I was far from lonely because my mind was totally engaged in the experience.

Although I could easily run a marathon a day for two days in a row, running the equivalent of two continuous marathons without stop proved to be much tougher than I'd imagined. The first half of the race went smoothly enough, despite the driving wind and mounting cold.

But during the second half, things started to deteriorate. The trauma to my body was much greater than I had anticipated, and the trail conditions worsened. As I stepped over tree roots and across icy puddles of mud, there came a point in the run, at about mile 38, where every muscle in my body was in pain. My fingers hurt, my forearms hurt, my shoulders ached, and of course my legs screamed in agony.

Early in the race I'd been downing solid food—peanut butter sandwiches, cheese, crackers—but now I was subsisting on cut fruit alone. My appetite was gone, but I forced myself to stomach the fruit to keep the energy level up. Pain has an odd way of suppressing hunger; when you most need the calories, food is entirely unappetizing.

For the first 43 miles, the run was entirely in the realm

of the physical, and pain was the dominant sensation. But then my mind started scurrying off on its own. Instead of being one continual impulse, the pain began to come and go like lightning. In between the jolts of pain were blissful, almost euphoric moments.

There was no way for me to control the onset of either sensation, no way to shift the balance from pain to pleasure. I tried holding my breath until I turned blue, tightening the muscles in my forearms in an attempt to pull the pain from my legs, running with my hands over my head—nothing worked. My body was on autopilot, and I was just along for the ride.

Despite this quasi-out-of-body experience, I kept trudging onward, ecstasy flirting with pain. The last 2 miles of the course were more about survival than running. I just shuffled along, step by step, barely able to lift my feet. After eight hours and twenty-seven minutes, I staggered across the finish line, 50 miles completed. "Victorious" is probably an overstatement. But it was a glorious moment nonetheless—I'd just qualified for the Western States 100!

On shaky legs, I stumbled to the finishers' tent and received a ribbon and a few handshakes and slaps on the back. Then I lumbered painfully to my car. When I plopped down on the leather seats, my legs went strangely cold. Something wasn't right. Then, without warning, the quadriceps and calf muscles of both legs seized in wicked cramps. My torso swung violently left, and then wildly back to the right. My legs were pegged to the floorboard, completely rigid. All ten toes were locked in place, force-fully curled against the soles of my shoes. My calf muscles were tight as baseballs, and my thighs were like solid planks of wood. The pain was mind-bending, pounding, entirely owning every drop of me.

Sweat poured down my face, and I screamed at the top of my lungs. Out of the corner of my eye I could see people casually strolling by my car, totally oblivious of the situation inside. Apparently the seals that were so effective at keeping noise out were also pretty good at keeping noise in. There was nothing I could do but scream: other than the ability to open my mouth, I was completely immobilized. I yelled louder and louder and louder, but no one outside could tell that I was inside on the verge of blowing apart.

My screaming was interrupted by a curious belch. Then came a few more burps. Something was rising up inside my stomach. Suddenly my mouth opened, and projectile vomit began streaming out. I tried to tilt my head downward toward the floorboard, but I was com-pletely incapable of altering the flow of things. I must have looked like Godzilla blowing fire into the air.

It lasted maybe thirty seconds. When I'd run dry, the entire dashboard and steering wheel were covered in vile sludge. The cramps were still so severe that all I could move were my eyeballs. The rest of my body felt like brittle glass. *What to do now?*

Perhaps if I could force my body into a different po-sition, the rigor mortis might be broken. With a few spasmodic jerks, I dislodged my left arm from the arm-rest. It fell to the floorboard like a piece of limp rubber, my hand flopping numbly to the plush carpet. Slowly walking my fingers back, I located the seat-adjustment buttons. The first button I pushed moved the seat forward, cramming my outstretched legs farther into the floorboard. This action sent a bolt of pain shooting up my body like an electrical shock. *Not good.* I quickly retracted my finger, and then moved it to the next button back. This lowered the headrest and began squashing my skull like a melon. By the time I was able to release the control, my head was wedged below the headrest and the seat back and I was feeling faint. *Really not good.*

With the third button, my upper body began to recline. Weird creaking and crackling noises resonated from my torso as I slid backward. As I approached horizontal, the pain began to ease. When the seat was fully reclined, I took my finger off the control and lay there motionless.

Now that I was in less agony, I could begin to assess the situation. Partially digested chunks of cantaloupe dripped from the steering column. I could sense dampness on my legs, but my entire lower torso was completely numb, so I really wasn't sure what was going on down there. I knew my next step was to get out of the car. Reaching up, I tugged on the door handle. At first it wouldn't yield, but with a more forceful jerk the latch unexpectedly released and the door swung open.

My upper body came flailing out of the car and my arms were too weak to buttress my fall, so I came crashing down face-first into the dirt. I lay splayed on the ground, half of my body outside of the car and my legs and feet still inside. My face rested in the dirt, and I watched little swirls of dust flowing out from under my nostrils with each exhalation. Though I must have looked utterly pathetic lying there, I could just as well have been standing on a podium having a medal placed over my head. After months of dedicated training and preparation, my goal had been achieved, my mission accomplished. It was a proud moment.

Eventually I was able to drag the rest of my body out of the car. My face was covered in dust and my clothes were filthy. My pride was intact, though, as I piloted the Lexus home, utilizing the cruise control to regulate my speed, too petrified to push on the pedals for fear that my legs would cramp again and I'd crash.

As for the car, it never was the same. But I began to appreciate the vehicle more now that it had been properly christened. We had lived through the worst, and our shared history brought us closer together. When my boss inquired about the rancid odor, I told him some fruit had rotted inside . . . which wasn't far from the truth.

Julie was thrilled to learn that I'd qualified for the Western States, although at first I didn't tell her about the little post-race episode in the car. She asked about the difficulty of running fifty miles nonstop, and I told her it was the hardest thing I'd ever done, by far. That's why I loved it.

When I told my parents that I was going to attempt to run 100 miles, their response was amazement. "Can you do it?" my mom asked.

"I'm not sure, that's why I want to try," I told her.

They had all kinds of questions and we talked at length about running, and about life. It was our most spirited conversation in years. My newfound love of running seemed to awaken a sense of hope. There was something in our future to look forward to; something, perhaps, grand and monumental. Attempting to run 100 miles was a spectacular aspiration, and the pursuit of this dream seemed to transcend career goals and other ambitions. My parents could sense my enthusiasm, and I could sense theirs. A flame had been ignited.

Chapter 6

Leaving Normal

*Two roads diverged in a wood, and I took
the one less traveled by.*

—Robert Frost

**The Bay Area
1993–1994**

To call running "fun" would be a misuse of the
word. Running can be "enjoyable." Running can be "rejuvenating." But in a pure sense of the word, running is
not fun.

After qualifying for the Western States, I ran every
chance I got. Mostly I ran early in the morning or late at
night. Sometimes I could squeeze in a run at lunch. But
just like most runners, running was something that had
to fit around my hectic work schedule, so it would be a
stretch to call it fun.

Now "entertaining" might more accurately describe things. Showing up for Monday-morning meetings after having run for the previous five hours was *entertaining*. Running a quick eight miles during lunch, and then changing in the backseat of my car, was *entertaining*. Running through places like Bentonville, Arkansas, and Lubbock, Texas, was, well, *entertaining* (and I'm glad to have escaped alive, given the many strange looks I received from people with gun racks in their pickups).

It was a schizophrenic existence—renegade extreme athlete on one hand, corporate loyalist on the other—but I was willing to do whatever it took, and I spent the balance of a year largely concealing my behavior from co-workers. Running was a passion; work paid the rent and Julie's dental-school bills. There would be no sacrificing my "company man" reputation for running. So I downplayed my running, uneasy that others might interpret an extracurricular interest of this intensity as a softening of my devotion to the company. A kink in the corporate armament.

Yet in my heart, my devotions were indeed shifting. Completing the Western States Endurance Run had become a goal as meaningful to me as any other in my life. Never before had I been so challenged by a single pursuit. Nor had I ever been so captivated and engaged. The training continued more fervently than ever, and I continued treading the delicate line between recklessness and responsibility, never letting on how much time and effort were being poured into this single dream.

Because of the demands of my work schedule, I trained primarily alone. It was too difficult to coordinate with other athletes, and training solo was actually enjoyable. Although I generally kept to myself about my running, I was beginning to get something of a "hell-man" reputation among my closest friends and colleagues who knew about it. It's difficult to keep such obsessions completely under wraps. Many of my nearest acquaintances were convinced that I was losing it, and subtly my circle of friends began to shift. My interests had changed, and I started meeting other ultra-athletes, like Pete Athens, who could empathize with my plight and who ultimately provided the inspiration for me to pursue my dream with total commitment.

Pete had scaled Mount Everest an unprecedented seven times, and he was preparing for his next expedition. No other Westerner had matched this feat. Though tougher than an ox, Pete was one of the most unassuming and humble individuals I'd ever met. His years of living so close to the edge had left him with a shaman-like wisdom.

In talking with Pete, it became clear to me that the Western States Endurance Run would be primarily about one thing: not giving up. It really didn't matter how long it took to get the job done; what mattered was getting it done. This was an exploration into the possibilities of self. Being a champion meant not quitting, no matter how tough the situation became, and no matter how badly the odds seemed stacked against you. If you had the courage, stamina, and persistence to cross the finish line, you were a champion.

The one dynamic that never got discussed with Pete was the question of "Why?" Why did he feel compelled to scale the highest mountains? What, exactly, was going on inside his head?

For that matter, what was going on inside mine?

For me, I knew, running great distances was a release; and, on some level, my boundless energy needed an outlet. The average obsessive-compulsive takes seven years to get help. The average runner covers 10,920 miles in that time. Whether my affliction was clinical is anyone's guess; I never did submit to testing. Some seek the comfort of their therapist's office, others head for the corner pub and dive into a pint, but I choose running as my therapy. It was the best source of renewal there was. I couldn't recall a single time that I felt worse after a run than before. What drug could compete? As Lily Tomlin said, "Exercise is for people who can't handle drugs and alcohol."

I'd also come to recognize that the simplicity of running was quite liberating. Modern man has virtually everything one could desire, but too often we're still not fulfilled. "Things" don't bring happiness. Some of my finest moments came while running down the open road, little more than a pair of shoes and shorts to my name. A runner doesn't need much. Thoreau once said that a man's riches are based on what he can do without. Perhaps in needing less, you're actually getting more.

But this goes way beyond running. There are deeper forces at play, darker and mysterious elements that are not so easily articulated.

When you get right down to it, the answer to "Why?" is a complex one. Why do people drink? Gamble? Fall in love? Short of psychoanalysis, I'm not sure how to get at these answers. Why my thing is running, I'm not certain. Plenty of people are discontent with their lives, but not many come to the conclusion that running for twenty-four hours straight will solve the problem.

Clearly it wasn't for the glory that I ran. The Western States Endurance Run was unknown to the general public. Unlike a typical big-city marathon or 10K, there would be no cheering fans lining the course, no corporate logos plastered along the way. At the Western States, I would spend most of my time running alone in the mountains, far removed from the fanfare and hype of a typical organized athletic event.

Why was I so compelled to push beyond all plausible limits of physical endurance to complete an endeavor that seemed so obscure and, some might say, irrational? I wasn't entirely sure myself. It's not that extreme athletes lack introspection; most whom I've encountered are quite reflective. It's just that the question of "Why?" is not a simple one to answer. The mechanics involved are complicated.

More often than not, the person asking "Why?" is looking for a brief psychobabble cliché to adequately explain the phenomenon, something like: "I run because when I was a kid, my father chased me out of the house and down the street with a belt in hand."

To those who asked me "Why?" I would frequently offer up some shallow explanation like "I enjoy running." What I guess I should have said was, "Go out and run fifty miles, then you'll have *your* answer."

Because I was still searching for *mine*.

Chapter 7

Over the Mountains and Through the Woods

Adventure is worthwhile in itself.

—Amelia Earhart

Lake Tahoe
Summer 1994

My mind was spinning during the days leading up to the Western States Endurance Run. Did I train hard enough? Should I have done more hill work? Damn, I forgot to submit that expense report. What was that odd sensation in my quad muscle? Wasn't that budget due tomorrow?

But then everything that was extraneous started to fade before the event itself. All of the external clutter, hurry, and noise started to melt away, and a radiant clarity began to emerge. With that came a singularity of purpose that is rarely experienced in our busy world. There are accounts of mountain climbers who encountered similar feelings. While preparing for the expedition, their mood was often frantic and disjointed. But once on the mountain, a lucid focus emerged out of the chaos. There was one clearly defined goal: making it to the summit.

One either made it to the top of the mountain or failed. Simple as that.

Life is rarely so neatly defined. Goals are often ambiguous and elusive. Seldom do people know exactly what is required of them to succeed. Often we think we're moving in the right direction only to learn that the rules have changed.

As daunting as it would be to run for twenty to thirty hours straight, at least I knew what was expected of me. There would be a starting line, and 100 miles from that a finish line. All I needed to do was run from here to there. No ambiguity about it. "We are at home in our games because it is the only place we know just what we are supposed to do," Albert Camus once said.

Although the task seemed incredibly difficult, at least the rules of engagement were clear. There were no hidden meanings or mixed messages. Just run, and don't stop. If I made it 100 miles, I'd succeed. If I didn't, I'd fail.

The Western States medical check-in

This revelation was going through my head as the medical assistant took my vitals. Medical check-in for the Western States takes place the day before the race. It was mandatory for all participants to have their weight and vital signs recorded. The information is printed on a hospital cuff that's attached to the runner's wrist. It cannot be removed until he or she either finishes the race or drops out from exhaustion (or is helevac'ed out by emergency rescue services).

The check-in was conducted at the base of the Squaw Valley ski resort. The scene was abuzz with energy as runners and crew scurried around making last-minute preparations for the race. Squaw Valley was the site of the 1960 Winter Olympic Games, and a regal aura still surrounds the resort. The Olympic torch is kept burning at the entrance. Everything at Squaw Valley looms larger than life. The trees are huge, the peaks massive, the Olympic rings are two stories high, and the flame of the torch burns like a bonfire surrounded by towering mountain ridges in every direction.

As you stand at the race check-in area, the bulk of the horizon is defined by colossal granite spires. To the east is KT-22 at 8,200 feet. Directly in your face is Squaw Peak at 8,900 feet. Slightly to the west is Emigrant Pass at 8,700. And Granite Chief commands the western skyline at 9,050 feet above sea level. It's an awesome sight to watch the gondola whisk up the steep cables toward the snow-covered cornice off in the heavens.

"That's where we go, you know," a voice resonated from behind me.

I turned to see a brawny man of about fifty staring up at the mountain through a pair of aviator sunglasses.

"Pardon me?" I said.

"That's where we go tomorrow," he said with a grin. I saw the hospital cuff around his wrist.

"You mean we run up to the top of the chairlift?" I asked.

"Hey-diddle-diddle, right up the middle," he said cheerfully. "It's a full frontal attack. We start here at the base, run right up the guts of this valley, traverse that ridge," he explained, pointing up at the ridge that defined the western horizon. "And then we crest the summit and start down the backside."

It seemed like a cruel way to start a 100-mile footrace. Just running the four miles from the base of the mountain to the summit would be brutal. The pitch of this four-mile climb was nearly straight up in certain sections—not to mention the distress of high altitude, with the summit looming some 9,000 feet above sea level. The air would be thin, and the footing would be a lousy mixture of loose rocks, melting snow, and thick mud.

"The name's Rock." He held out his hand. "At least that's what my friends call me."

I introduced myself.

"This your first States, son?" Rock asked.

I nodded slowly. "How could you tell?"

"That's easy." He lifted his shirt to reveal a shining silver belt buckle. It was beautifully ornate, with a golden cougar highlighted in the middle. Printed on it were the words: 100 MILES, ONE DAY. Like everything else around here, the buckle was huge.

"You're not wearing one of these," Rock went on, "and you look damn capable, so I figured you'd have one of these bad boys if you'd done the race before."

That was a fine compliment. To earn the Silver Buckle, you not only had to complete the course, but do it in under twenty-four hours. The silver belt-buckle prize was a carryover from the event's humble beginnings as a horse race. It was arguably the most cherished endurance running award on the planet. Only a portion of the starters tomorrow would earn one.

Two other runners strolled up and stopped abruptly in front of Rock.

"Sir!" they barked.

Rock turned to them slowly. "Hello, boys," he said with a wide grin. They nodded to him sharply and then turned and continued on their path.

It was the pair who'd passed me on Lovers' Lane and inadvertently introduced me to this *sport*. We had *met* at the top of Lovers' Lane, exchanged pleasantries at the fifty-mile qualifying run (at least *I* had said hello), and here again they'd ignored me. I was beginning to feel more insulted by these guys. It must've shown on my face.

"Don't mind them," Rock said. "They're just doing their job."

"And just what job is that?" I asked.

"Well . . ." Rock hesitated. "Let's just say they're in the military."

"So they can't introduce themselves?"

"Well . . ." Rock paused again. "Let's just say they're in a *special* kind of military. And they can't introduce themselves. Actually, they *could*, but they'd just give you an alias, so what's the difference?"

"You mean to tell me they can't even acknowledge my presence?" I smirked. "How they gonna make any friends acting like that?"

Rock grinned. "They already have all the friends they need, each other. Everybody else is considered a potential enemy."

"That's comforting."

"Don't take it personally. It's just how they're trained to think."

Rock grasped my shoulder firmly. "Listen, stay focused on the task at hand. Don't get distracted by those other guys. You're not competing against anyone but yourself. I want to see you at that finish line with a buckle in hand."

"Yes, sir!" I barked.

Rock smiled.

My parents volunteered to help crew for me during the run and had made the nine-hour drive up from Southern California. The Western States Endurance Run would be an adventure for all three of us. Unfortunately, Julie couldn't be with us because her State Dental Board examinations fell on the same weekend. These tests would be the final hurdle in her quest to become a licensed dentist. She had been nothing but supportive of my own quest, and I had made my best attempt to be equally supportive of her dream to become a dentist. But this time there was, unfortunately, no alternative but for her to do her thing and me mine.

I met my parents in the lobby of the Inn at Squaw Creek, a beautiful resort at the base of the mountain. After my sister's death a decade before, our get-togethers could sometimes be strained. There were so many feelings, so many thoughts that were never expressed. But now, standing in this grand foyer with the mountains surrounding us, we were at ease with one another as we chuckled at the opulence of the surroundings, which seemed so incongruous with the journey I was about to embark on the next morning.

The full extent of my reborn passion for running had not been obvious to my parents until this meeting. News about my running came to them in sporadic phone calls and brief mentions in letters I wrote. We didn't spend as much time together as we should have. But now, as they saw me lean and focused, perpetually sipping from a water bottle, the scope of my transformation was evident.

"You look great," my dad said enthusiastically.

My mom smiled. "This is so exciting."

A black-tie event was taking place at the Inn, and elegant women and tuxedoed men filled the lobby. It was an older crowd, perhaps the retirement party of some elder statesman or local dignitary. A little stiff for my liking, but fun to watch from a distance. Suddenly, there was a deafening roar just outside the building. A woman shrieked and dropped her martini. The crowd went into a conniption, people scurried left and right, not sure whether to stay put or flee. I looked out and saw a huge green Humvee pull up to the front of the hotel. The thing was massive and roared like a tank. It was caked with mud and had a wheelbase that could easily have swallowed two or three of the nearby Jaguars.

The driver swung open the door and jumped down to the parking lot. He was dressed in a leather pilot's jacket—and running shorts. His legs were like gnarled tree stumps. He opened the passenger door and hauled out an alligator-skin briefcase. Then he reached behind the seat and pulled out a big rifle. And I mean a *big* rifle. He slung this over his shoulder and, with the engine still thundering at idle, strolled up to the reservation counter as though nothing were amiss. He rested one elbow on the countertop and chatted with the young receptionist. She said something that made him throw back his head and laugh—though you could barely hear him over his rumbling H1. She handed him his room key, and he walked casually down the lavish hallway, rifle and all.

Eventually one of the valets drove the vehicle off.

"That was one hell of an entrance," my dad said.

"I wonder what he'll do for an encore," I replied.

Later, we enjoyed a nice dinner on the patio. The night air was warm and still, which wasn't necessarily a good thing. Weather tomorrow would be a major factor, especially in the deep canyons along the middle of the course, where midday temperatures could easily hit triple digits. Along the course would be a series of aid stations and checkpoints, but most would be little more than a few guys handing out water and encouragement. Most runners carry food and liquid with them, an added burden but necessary to remain hydrated and nourished. Crunching a few pieces of ice on the patio that evening, I relished a luxury that would be in short supply the next day.

Sleep didn't come easy that night. I tossed and turned and was wide awake when the alarm went off at 3:00 A.M. My parents were soon stumbling around the room half-asleep, helping me go down my checklist:

➤ Fill water bottles
➤ Put on sunscreen
➤ Band-Aid nipples (to prevent chafing)
➤ Sprinkle baby powder on the feet (to prevent blistering)
➤ Drink eight glasses of water (to superhydrate)

- ➤ Take 1,000 mg of vitamin C (no particular reason, just seemed prudent)
- ➤ Apply lubricant to critical areas
- ➤ Prepare fanny pack with food and supplies

That done, my parents went into the bathroom—trying to wake up, I presumed—until music filled the room. The theme to *Zorba the Greek* shook the walls, and my folks burst out in makeshift hotel-towel togas. They started Greek-dancing across the room and over the bed, whirling and cheering with zeal. I jumped into the fray, and the three of us danced like kids at our first pajama party. At the conclusion we let out a collective *"Oppa!"* It was the Greek version of reveille.

When we arrived at the starting area, a pancake breakfast was in full swing. It felt odd sitting in a crowded cafeteria at 3:30 in the morning, mowing down a tall stack of pancakes like it was the corner IHOP on a busy Saturday morning. The peculiarity of the setting didn't dampen my appetite, however, and I scarfed down several mounds. Other runners filed nervously in and out. The coffee was black and thick as motor oil: perfect.

At 4:30, a horn sounded. I took one last gulp of coffee and we made our exit. The outside mountain air was crisp and laced with the scent of fresh pine. It was still pitch-black. Near the starting gate, racers and crew made the final adjustments to their equipment and went over their game plans. The crowd was primarily comprised of family, friends, and the occasional reporter. Beams from flashlights and headlamps haphazardly dissected the predawn sky like miniature searchlights. I checked in with a race official, who simply said, "Good luck."

There was a string of Tibetan prayer flags hung over the start, and a long white ribbon was tied across the dirt trail. Staring up at the granite mountaintops now visible in the predawn light, I thought about my sister Pary and how happy she would be knowing that I was pursuing a dream, doing something I loved. I hugged Mom and Dad and took my place in the crowd of runners.

A loudspeaker crackled to life—*"Ten minutes until race start!"*—and the fidgeting, preoccupied crowd went absolutely berserk, whistling and howling like beasts. Runners bounced up and down, spun around, shook their arms wildly. The guy next to me started shadow-boxing with the mountains.

A man strolled out of the darkness in running shorts and a leather jacket, with a *big* rifle slung over his shoulder: the Humvee driver. He walked casually yet deliberately toward the starting line; it was clear the encore was about to begin.

He hopped up onto a large rock beside the starting line, and all eyes focused on him as he turned to face the crowd. His voice rang clear in the still morning air:

"First of all," he said, "I want to congratulate every one of you for having the courage to be standing here at the starting line of this incredible event. To have made it this far, and to have had the dedication and drive to be at this point, represents a tremendous accomplishment in its own right.

"Many of you will not reach the finish line. I applaud your efforts and your determination. Even though you do not finish this event, you will walk away a winner for having the courage to have tried.

"For those of you who do make it, you will cross that finish line as a different person. You will be forever changed by the experience. You will learn more about yourself in the next day than you have previously known in an entire lifetime."

My body may have been conditioned like a thoroughbred, but it was evident from his words that this would be more than a physical journey.

Over the loudspeaker came: *"Five minutes until race start."*

The man with the rifle unfolded a sheet of paper and began to read: "'My fair cousin; if we are mark'd to die, we are honored by our country in its tragic loss. And if we live, the fewer men, the greater the share of honor.'"

The morning air swirled around the crowd and the sky seemed to rumble.

"'God's will, I pray thee, not one more man. For I am not covetous for gold, nor care I for material flourishments. But if it be a sin to covet honor, I am the most offending soul alive. We few, we happy few, we band of brothers; for he today that sheds his blood with me shall be my brother.'"

It was an excerpt from Shakespeare's King Henry V's rallying cry to his weary soldiers before the battle of Agincourt.

The loudspeaker blared: *"One minute until race start."*

The guy with the rifle continued: "'He that outlives this day, and comes safe home, will stand a tiptoe above all others. Old men forget; yet all shall be forgot, but he'll remember, with advantages, what feats he did this day. This story shall the good man teach his son, and forever in their flowing cups will it be remembered; from this day to the ending of the world!'"

"Ten seconds until race start," boomed the loudspeaker. *"Nine, eight, seven . . ."*

The rifle-toting man pointed his weapon skyward.

". . . six, five, four . . ."

At the stroke of zero he pulled the trigger, and a mighty blast shook the air. The ribbon dropped, and, for a second, time seemed suspended. The shot echoed up the valley and then back down again.

Over the loudspeaker came a farewell diktat: "CHAAARGE!!"

The adventure had begun.

Chapter 8

King of Pain

> *That which does not kill you*
> *makes you stronger.*
>
> —Friedrich Nietzsche

Sierra Nevada
5:01 A.M., June 25, 1994

The 379 runners charged forward in a pack. The crowd roared. Flashbulbs ignited the cloud of dust we kicked up. I was desperately trying not to step on or be stepped on by anyone in the middle of the horde. The race was on.

As we pounded up the mountain, the pack quickly thinned; stronger runners pulled ahead, weaker ones fell behind. I remained somewhere in the middle. I'd been told that one of the tricks to finishing the Western States—though I questioned whether there was any such thing as a "trick" to running 100 miles—was not to start out too hard. If you go out too fast, your muscles don't get the oxygen they need to run efficiently. This causes a buildup of lactic acid in the muscles that can later bring swelling and pain, even temporary paralysis.

So I was taking a reserved and consistent approach to the first several miles of the race. The climb up to Emigrant Pass was so steep that I was forced to move very slowly anyway. The high altitude and thin air didn't help my pace much, either.

It felt weird running up slopes I'd snowboarded down many times in the winter. At the summit of Emigrant Pass is the peak of Granite Chief. At 9,050 feet, it towers over the surrounding mountains. Getting up to Granite Chief as a skier requires three separate and lengthy chairlift rides. We ran under these lifts as we climbed.

Three miles up the course, I looked back down the winding valley. There was a steady procession of runners moving up the trail like pack mules. The field had spread considerably, and most were now in single file. Above, the first golden rays of sunlight were lighting up Granite Chief. It was like the opening round of a title fight, my opponent being a 9,000-foot mountain.

Soon I began experiencing the effects of the high altitude. My head grew light, and the surrounding scenery started to look dreamlike and distant. My fingers swelled so that I had difficulty opening and closing my hands. In the Official Participants Guide, a binder issued to every runner, an entire chapter is devoted to "Medical and Other Risk Factors." It noted: "The high altitude plus exertion can produce various degrees of mountain (altitude) sickness. This can lead to severe lung and brain swelling, and even death." It had been a little unsettling to see the use of the D-word. I could accept—and expect—severe discomfort or even hospitalization, but brain swelling and death were a bit much. Sure, I wanted to finish this event, but the idea of dying in the process wasn't too appealing.

Still, I kept pushing forward at a steady pace. Nearing the crest, I encountered something unexpected: snow. Large swatches of it crossed the trail, and the entire summit was covered. The footing was unstable; it was difficult to put any power into my stride without slipping. There were big foot-holes along the snow-path where other runners had stepped too heavily and broken through the flimsy crust. I slowed to prevent falling. Several runners were attempting to pass me, but it was easy to posthole in the untracked snow and slip (potentially a long way down). So, demoralizing as it was, I did the courteous thing and stepped aside to let them pass. No one thanked me for this show of sportsmanship; they just kept motoring along as though I wasn't even there.

I reminded myself that at this stage of the race, anyone could run strong. But what toll would it take farther down the line? Long-distance running requires a certain discretion and reserve. It's easy to let your ego get the better of you early on and run beyond your means. It's a mistake that may haunt you as the miles and the hours add up. One of my biggest challenges in this early stage would be to have the discipline to go slow, even as other runners passed me. And I hated being passed.

When I neared the summit, called the Escarpment, a short line of runners was waiting to get water at the first aid station. I pulled up to the back of the line and bent over, my hands on my knees, breathing deeply. I couldn't catch my breath in the thin air.

Somebody tapped me on the shoulder. One of the aid-station volunteers stood next to me with a pitcher of water.

"Can I fill your bottles?" he asked.

Without looking up, I said, "Sure."

In my hip pack were two 16-ounce water bottles. Both had been full at the start of the race. I'd emptied them—a quart of water—in 4 miles.

"Where you from?" the volunteer asked as he filled them.

"San Francisco."

"Ah . . . that's a very nice place," he said. "But you best be on your way."

"Why's that? I'd like to enjoy the view for a moment," I replied, jokingly—I was still hunched over looking straight down at the dirt.

"Well, there's one thing I'm sure about San Francisco," he went on. "It's at sea level. Let me see your hands."

I held out my right hand and he squeezed my fingers.

"Your best move at this point would be to get up over that summit and start heading down to lower elevation," he advised. "Once you get over the pass, the trail starts to descend quickly. You're not going to be able to catch your breath standing here, no matter how long you stay. We're too high up in the sky."

He was right. I took one last deep breath and stood straight up.

"Thanks, partner," I said.

"Just doing my job," he replied. "Now get out of here."

I started moving forward again. The summit was only seven-tenths of a mile away—unfortunately, though, it was nearly straight up. My watch said it was 6:09 A.M. The time of day for a projected twenty-four-hour pace at this point was 6:05 A.M., so I was right on target. But then again, I was a very short distance into a very long race.

Today I would rely on my watch like never before. I'd still run with my heart, but I'd need to use my head as well. I'd use my watch to make sure my pace was sensible.

Even without referencing the time, though, it was clear that my tempo to the summit was arduously slow. At several points I was on all fours, literally crawling up through the snow, as were other runners around me. It was extremely slippery and very steep, and there wasn't much to hold on to. My fingers were turning blue from the cold. Other runners had on gloves, but I hadn't thought to bring a pair.

When I finally did claw my way to the summit and check my watch, the time was 7:01 A.M. It had taken me 52 minutes to go less than a mile. At that pace, the entire race would take four and one-half days to complete. I pushed another button on my watch and got a temperature read: 38 degrees Fahrenheit.

The views from the summit, however, were enough to alleviate some of the brutality of the climb. It was breathtaking in every direction. The sun had now made its way into the sky, and beams of silvery light were dancing across Lake Tahoe in the distance. I was standing on the highest peak in the surrounding area. Below was a line of runners trekking up the narrow trail cut into the mountainside. Encircling me were other towering snow-covered peaks jabbing the sky for as far as the eye could see.

Another runner was admiring the view. The man was rugged and chiseled and looked like a seasoned veteran.

"Where do we go from here?" I inquired.

He scanned the horizon to the west. "See that peak over there?" He pointed to a very distant mountain, maybe 20 miles away.

"Yes, I see it."

"Okay. Once we get there, the finish is seventy-five miles beyond that point."

He was trying to be encouraging, I think, but the enormity of what we were doing gripped me. We had covered about five miles, and the peak he was pointing

at was about twenty miles away. Another 75 miles beyond that would make 100.

The math was logical, yet seeing it all laid out in front
of me for the first time was overwhelming. Just making
it to that first distant peak looked daunting. It was barely
visible on the horizon. There would be untold battles
waged along the trail just to reach that peak 20 miles
away. And from there, ". . . the finish is about seventy-
five miles . . ." It seemed unfathomable.

I thanked him for the perspective and pressed on. My
approach to running 100 miles would be little different
from running a 10K: I'd simply put one foot in front of
the other and not stop until I crossed the finish line.
Hopefully.

Emigrant Pass to Robinson Flat
Miles 4.7 to 30.2

Running downhill felt good, much easier than the
climb up. The challenge now became not slipping in the
uneven snow. Back-country snow on west-facing ridges
doesn't melt uniformly. Little pockets of menacing "sun-
cups" form, with narrow pinnacles and foot-swallowing
troughs. The best method for traversing a field of sun-
cups is to use an accelerated tiptoe-style run to minimize
contact with the pitted surface. Still, even with this adap-
tive running technique, it was hard to avoid falling and

sliding downhill. I watched as some runners slid a good twenty feet down the mountainside. I fell several times myself.

My second big challenge was wet socks. That's not as insignificant as it may sound. Other runners wore gaiters over their shoes to keep the snow out, but I hadn't thought of that. Snow seeped in, melted, and soaked my socks.

By the time I reached the Lion Ridge aid station sixteen miles from the start, the damp, softened skin of my feet was already starting to blister. Blisters can become so painful that they force an athlete out of the race. A scant sixteen miles into it, my mind was dwelling on the letters DNF: DID NOT FINISH. More than a third of the field would be listed as DNF tomorrow. I did not want to be one of them because of destroyed feet. But there was little I could do about it until I reached the Robinson Flat medical checkpoint, at mile 30, which was the first access point for support crew, and where my parents would have fresh socks waiting.

It was a long slog to get there. Most of the trail was still above 7,000 feet, and where the snow ended, water and mud took over. There were switchbacks that led to more switchbacks that ended in abrupt uphills or downhills. And the trail was littered with natural debris. The snowmelt had dragged rocks, trees, roots, and big chunks of earth across the path. You had to do a lot of jumping over and climbing around. My poor wet feet got more and more tender. Going downhill hurt the worst, as my feet slid forward, mashing my toes against the fronts of my shoes.

And then I came to the first of many river crossings. The water, cold and crisp, came up to above my knees. I splashed some on my face and neck. It actually felt good, even though it was still early in the morning and fairly cool out.

Hours passed, miles were covered, and eventually the distance totaled 30 miles. Coming around the corner and into the Robinson Flat aid station is like discovering an oasis. One second you're on a remote trail in the middle of the mountains. Then you pop around a random corner, and mystically this little city of bustling commerce appears. There are a number of white tents set up for shelter, and lots of fresh food and cold drinks. From a runner's perspective, after you've run thirty miles through the wilderness, Robinson Flat is a welcome sight.

I was quickly ushered to the medical checkpoint. They put me on a scale and informed me that I'd lost about a pound so far. The rules state:

Vital signs will be checked at various points along the trail. Weight loss will be one of the most important of these physiological criteria to be evaluated. A loss of 3% of one's body weight indicates that significant dehydration has occurred. At 5% weight loss, a runner may be nearly exhausted and will be scrutinized closely by the medical staff. A 7% loss of body weight will be grounds for mandatory withdrawal from the run, due to the high risk of heat exhaustion, hypothermia, and increasing risk of dangerous impairment of body functions.

With just one pound shed so far, I was fine. However, I'd covered less than a third of the race. It would be important to keep hydrated and nourished to avoid losing critical body mass and risk "dangerous impairment of body functions," whatever that meant (it certainly didn't sound good).

As I stepped off the scale and walked toward the medical aid area, people were clapping and patting me on the back. "You look great!" "Way to go!" "Keep it up." There were a couple of other runners seated in the medical area having their feet examined. I exchanged nods and took the farthest seat down in the row. It was nothing more than a flimsy beach chair, but it felt like a plush leather sofa.

"How are the feet?" a volunteer asked.

"I'm not sure," I said. "They're pretty wet and they feel a little tender, especially between my toes."

He knelt. "Let's get those shoes off and have a look." He removed my right shoe and held it upside down to let the water stream out. My foot was white as a marshmallow and looked as though it had been soaking for hours. There were huge fissures and crags along the entire length. But perhaps most disturbing was the acorn-size blister between my big and second toes.

Just then my parents rushed over to me.

"Hello, son," my dad said. "How's it going so far?"

"So far, so good," though I caught a look of concern when he saw my swollen, disfigured foot.

The volunteer, Jim, continued to inspect my feet carefully, top and bottom. "I'm going to need to lance these blisters to relieve some of the pressure. It shouldn't take long, but it might sting a little."

"How are we going to stop the skin from pulling away?" I asked.

"That's a good question," he said. "After I've lanced the blister, I'm going to stick the skin together and then tape it to prevent further damage."

"Are you sure this is the best way to approach it?"

Jim nodded. "Trust me on this one. I've done it a hundred times."

Before I could really comprehend what was happening, he tore off the wrapping from a small sterile scalpel and took aim at the blister on my right foot. Instantly there was a stream of serum running down my foot. Then the pain hit me. I winced and groaned through grinding teeth. There were beads of sweat rolling off my upper lip. Jim lanced another blister in this same manner. I felt light-headed and nauseated.

And then, amazingly, he pulled out a tube of Krazy Glue. He whipped off the red cap and inserted the tip of the tube into my blister. Then he produced a roll of duct tape. I was stunned. He was actually sealing my blisters with Krazy Glue and duct tape! I felt like a life raft having a leak repaired.

Still, I was better off than the runner who'd collapsed into a chair nearby and promptly fallen unconscious. People scurried around him, trying to support his head and prevent him from tumbling to the ground. A volunteer had a stethoscope pressed to the man's chest. She called to Jim, "Dr. Williams, we're going to need you over here."

He stood up. "Okay, get those clean socks on and you're good to go. Nice meeting you both," he said to my folks, who were standing there in a trance, and then to me, "I'll see you in Auburn."

Robinson Flat to Devil's Thumb
Miles 30.2 to 47.8

It was 11:44 A.M. when I officially checked out from the Robinson Flat aid station. The projected pace of a twenty-four-hour runner exiting Robinson Flat was 11:30 A.M. (though I was becoming less concerned about maintaining a twenty-four-hour finishing pace and more about just trying to hold it all together). I was the 124th runner to leave the checkpoint.

After Robinson Flat, the trail widened considerably. There were even long stretches of graded fire-road. Towering pine trees lined much of the trail, their bristles laying a soft blanket of mulch over the dirt for a cushioned landing. As I ran, I found myself instinctively favoring either the left or right side of the trail, never running down the middle. At first I thought this was because the bristle buildup was denser along the sides of the trail and the cushioning was advantageous. Then it dawned on me that it was getting hot; swerving side to side was an intuitive attempt to stay in the shade of the big pines.

My pace picked up on this more gentle terrain; however, running faster generated more body heat, and by the time I reached the Deep Canyon aid station at mile 35.8, I was drenched with sweat. I paused there only long enough to refill my water bottles and grab a handful of pretzels, wanting to get as far along the trail as possible before the real heat kicked in.

The only way out of Deep Canyon is to run up the other side. The uphill was savage, and the enveloping heat was becoming merciless. Every pore in my body now gushed sweat, and it was impossible to stay cool in the still, stifling air.

At several points along the trail were some peculiar watermarks in the dirt—periodic squiggles of wetness, fifteen to twenty feet long, as though someone had been aspirating his water bottle, which made no sense in this heat, where the goal was to conserve water, not squirt it out on the trail. These puzzled me until I came up behind another runner and saw the source. Let's just say it was a time-saving strategy: instead of stopping to relieve themselves, as I had done at least a half-dozen times so far, others were peeing on the run. They looked ridiculous doing it, but I had to concede that I'd probably lost five minutes so far pausing to do it the old-fashioned way. So I decided to adopt the technique and found that peeing on the run takes practice. It's not something they taught us in the Boy Scouts. You can't look down at what you're doing or you risk running off a cliff, spritzing all the way down. You have to keep your gaze on the trail and aim by instinct. I had a number of false starts—kind of like stage fright—but eventually got the hang of it, so to speak.

The sun beat down ruthlessly upon the trail as I progressed, heating the dirt and making every footstep uncomfortable. At the Dusty Corners aid station, mile 40, I showed the first disturbing sign of mild dehydration: my speech was slurred when I spoke to the volunteer who was sponging me down. He guided me to the nearby food table, where I promptly gobbled down every salty piece of food in sight: chips, pretzels, peanuts. My stomach full, I felt slightly more coherent.

When I thanked him, my speech had come back . . . a minor victory in a major war. Departing Dusty Corners, a bit shaken but still determined, I started singing:

"There's a little black spot on the sun today . . . I will always be King of Pain . . ." Odd that these lyrics popped to mind.

The trail turned into a gradual downslope, but now there was little shade to hide in. On the horizon, a pronounced layer of haze draped down into the valleys, hugging the topography as far as the eye could see. A balmy summer day in the Sierra foothills was in progress.

I felt pretty good, mentally and physically, when I pulled into the Last Chance checkpoint—mile 43.3— about a half-hour later. I had broken through a mental wall after Dusty Corners and was now in an up zone.

It was surprising to find that I was the only runner at the Last Chance checkpoint. There were at least a hundred runners somewhere in front of me, and probably twice that number behind me. Over the stretch of forty-three miles, though, we had become really spread out along the trail. I grabbed a handful of peanuts as one of the volunteers filled my water bottles. He was a young kid, probably no older than seventeen. His name was Nate—at least that's what his tattoo said.

"How ya doing?" I asked.

"Okay. It's pretty warm," he said, putting the cap back on my water bottle. "You'd better load up on water, there ain't much between here and Devil's Thumb."

Devil's Thumb was the crest on the other side of the canyon I was about to traverse, five miles away.

"Any reports on what it's like down there?"

"It's nasty: real hot and not much air movement. Wanna soak your shirt before leaving?"

I took off my shirt and tossed it into the water bucket. "You look pretty good," he said. "Some of the people coming through here are trashed. No way they're going to make it to Auburn."

I nodded, fully aware that soon enough I could be just as bad off.

"Good luck, man," he said, as I headed back out to the long and dusty trail.

The plunge into Deadwood Canyon was horrendously steep, with frequent curves and sharp corners to contend with; and it was roasting hot, even going downhill. The abrupt descent was followed, inevitably, by another uphill climb—an agonizing, hour-long struggle in the stifling heat. Rounding a particularly steep corner, I caught up with a runner who was obviously in serious trouble—hunched over, barely shuffling his feet in the dust. His side covered in dirt, clearly he had fallen. I pulled up beside him.

"How's it going?"

He didn't have the strength to raise his head. He just sort of turned his chin to make contact with one eye. There was a pale white froth around his mouth, and when he first tried to speak the words were nearly inaudible.

"I've felt better," he croaked.

We shuffled along together for a minute or so in the suffocating heat.

"Listen," I finally said, "I'm going to push on up to the aid station. Do you want me to send someone back for you?"

After a long pause he mumbled, "For me? Naw, don't send anybody back for me. Let them save their efforts for someone who really needs help."

A wild grin spread across his face. The guy was tough as nails. He knew he didn't have a chance to make it another 53 miles. Still, his spirit wasn't broken. He'd probably keep going until they carried him out on a gurney.

Devil's Thumb to Foresthill
Miles 47.8 to 62

It was 101 degrees when I reached the Devil's Thumb checkpoint. There was hardly a breath of air, and the heat radiated from the red clay soil in lazy, undulating ripples. Motionless runners lay strewn about the place like a scene from an old war movie—one in which the enemy was winning.

A volunteer waved me over to a scale. I'd now lost nearly three pounds, about 2 percent of my body weight. Other runners had lost more and were trying to rehydrate.

Maintaining proper hydration in such extreme conditions is tricky. It's essential to drink lots of water but also imperative to monitor your sodium intake. If you consume too much water and not enough sodium, or vice versa, you can easily throw your electrolytes out of balance; it's a downward spiral from that point.

I washed down a handful of pretzels with some Cytomax, an electrolyte replacement and lactic-acid-buffering solution popular with endurance athletes. Next to the pretzels sat a bowl of chopped potatoes, a dish of water, and a tub of salt. The idea was to dip the potato in water and then in salt. It tasted nasty, but it was an effective way to stomach a large quantity of sodium.

The next checkpoint beyond Devil's Thumb would be Michigan Bluff at mile 55.7. Unfortunately, between the two points was a 2,600-foot drop, followed by a merciless 2,000-foot climb.

Departing Devil's Thumb at 3:31 P.M., I was now just one minute behind my dream pace of a sub-twenty-four-hour finish. Still, after ten hours of continuous running, I hadn't yet even reached the halfway point. There was plenty of trail left to either make me or break me. It made little sense to be preoccupied with my time when there were no assurances that I'd ever reach the finish line.

The descent from Devil's Thumb was so steep at points that I had to turn sideways and sidestep downward. My shoes quickly filled with dirt and gravel, adding to the miserable soreness of my feet. Somewhere along this descent I passed the halfway point in the race. The milestone went unnoticed. It has been said of the Western States Endurance Run that you run the first 50 miles with your legs, and the last 50 miles with your mind. My mental toughness would now be tested like never before.

El Dorado Creek, at mile 52.9, marks the bottom of the gorge. The climb from El Dorado Creek up to Michigan Bluff was the harshest yet. At times I was crawling up the rocks on all fours, drenched in sweat, my legs so heavy and burdensome I could barely clear the natural debris that littered the trail. Periodically I would stumble on a rock or a branch. The hill just kept going on, and on, and on. The climb took an hour and a half.

Finally I could hear the distant voices of the pit crew at Michigan Bluff. As I came around one final twist in the trail, the checkpoint emerged through the brush. The last few steps took all my remaining energy. People were whirling around me, asking questions and offering kudos, but it all sounded like gibberish. My head was spinning, the words not registering as they should. It took tremendous effort just to remain standing. Everything appeared fuzzy and gyrating, and it felt as though I were chewing on a mouthful of lemon peels.

A volunteer poured ice water over my head. The frigid liquid shocked me. I shivered spastically, unable to control my twitching muscles.

Eventually I was able to regain my senses, and they brought me over to the scales. I was down over four pounds—probably even more, since my soaked clothes added some weight to the reading. This wasn't good.

It took me a while to regroup at Michigan Bluff. People brought me food and cold water, which helped— though I declined to take a seat that was offered, fearing I wouldn't be able to get back up. The food allowed me to regain some of my strength, and the camaraderie of so many supportive volunteers was a powerful tonic. When I checked out of the Michigan Bluff aid station, the crowd cheered, whistled, and clapped. It was an uplifting send-off.

Within minutes of departing the checkpoint, however, I found myself alone again on the trail. It was just after 5:20 P.M., and the next checkpoint, at Foresthill, was six short but tough miles away. *Just one 10K*, I thought to myself. *When I reach Foresthill, I'll have covered 62 miles*. From that point, all I would have left is a marathon and two back-to-back 10Ks. When exhaustion sets in, the mind often rationalizes the irrational.

The trail began a twisting descent into Volcano Canyon, another steep downhill with tight cornering and tricky footing. It required heightened attention to detail to prevent stumbling. Every step needed to be executed with precision and forethought. After descending a good thousand feet in two miles, I reached the pit of Volcano Canyon. It was utterly stifling down there, the hot air thick as stew. The water in my bottles was warm and tasted like plastic. As much as I needed water, it was difficult to stomach more than a sip or two of the now-foul liquid. Stumbling on the stones of an almost-dry creekbed, I put my hand down to catch my fall and nearly burned myself on a rock. Water leaked from my bottle, sizzling when it hit the ground and forming a little sauna-like puff of steam.

From the dry riverbed, it was an agonizing 4-mile climb up to the next checkpoint at Foresthill. Somewhere along this climb, maybe when the clump of dirt-encrusted sweat entered my eye, it grimly occurred to me again that I might not be able to complete the event. DNF kept flashing in my mind: DID NOT FINISH. If I allowed my spirit to weaken, I was sunk. A positive out-look was my greatest asset at this point. Despite being in the best shape of my life, no amount of brawn could carry me through another 40 miles. The real battle was inside my head.

Covering the last bit of distance into Foresthill, I found myself in a defensive, survival-like mode, stressing about my cramping thighs and dehydration, worrying about what the trail might throw at me next. The elements were beating me into submission. How was I possibly going to hold it together for the last 38 miles?

Fear, I thought to myself, just another four-letter word; but now as great an adversary as any mountain left before me. From here on in, the battle would be within.

Chapter 9

Into Darkness

What counts in battle is what you do
when the pain sets in.

—John Short

Foresthill, California
6:22 P.M., June 25, 1994

Running into Foresthill was like stepping out of a
train wreck and into a raging party. The path was lined
with people, many in costumes, beer steins in hand,
cheering and dancing on every side of me as I hobbled
down the approach.

Foresthill is the biggest checkpoint along the course.
It's easily accessible by car, and people come from all of
the small outposts around the area to join the festivities.
There was country music blaring, high-octane libations
flowing, and samples of PowerBars being handed out. It

was a weird mix of superathletic types and boisterous locals. Everyone seemed lit, for one reason or another.

A volunteer led me over to the scales. "How you doing?" she asked.

"I've felt better," I said, "but overall, things still seem to be working."

She chuckled. "You look great. Let's just record your weight and we'll send you on your way."

I stepped up on the scale.

"You're down almost five pounds," she observed, without much concern. "You're really going to have to maintain your fluid intake to prevent further dehydration. Try to take in a good amount of cold liquid before leaving this checkpoint. It's gonna be real hot along the next section of trail."

Like I've been running across Iceland, I thought, as I walked back onto the course. People were shouting encouragements and trying to give me high fives . . . only I couldn't lift my hand beyond shoulder level.

Many of the athletes have pacers who run the last 38 miles with them, beginning here at Foresthill. Pacers are not allowed to offer physical assistance, but they can give a lot of psychological encouragement. I didn't know anyone capable, let alone willing, to run with me for such a distance.

A race official asked if I had a pacer that would be joining me.

"I'm going it alone, brother," I said to him. "Unless you want to join me."

"What, and leave this party?" he grinned.

My parents were waiting for me at Foresthill. They guided me toward a little chair they had set up. I plopped in it, arms falling over the sides, and let out a groan. It was only the second time I had sat down in thirteen hours.

"How's it going, son?"

"Oh," I said, "it's going . . . it's going."

They opened the family Igloo cooler to reveal a treasure . . . sandwiches, fruit, crackers, and jelly beans, all of which I mashed by the handful into my mouth.

It was approaching 6:30 P.M., yet the sun still shone brightly. I sat there wolfing down food and taking a mental inventory of my condition. Luckily, my guts were relatively stable—other runners had reportedly dropped out from heat-related nausea. My feet, on the other hand, were toast. They were battered beyond repair; I'd just have to deal with the discomfort for the rest of the race. Not a lot of options there. My neck and shoulder muscles were tight, though not to the point of grave concern. My thighs were a different story. The juncture where my quadriceps connected to my hip was extremely tender on both sides of my body. The simple act of sitting down in a chair was excruciating. I rubbed the area in hopes of getting some relief, but the slightest pressure increased the pain. When it was time to move on, my folks had to help me out of the chair. My mom stuffed a sandwich and the rest of the jelly beans into my pack, and my dad topped off my water bottles.

"I'll see you kids on down the road," I said, trying to

remain optimistic, and began the painful transition from standing still to once again running.

"We love you, son," my mom said as I staggered off into the distance. "Good luck."

My steps were short and choppy at first, but slowly I eased into a moderate jog. It took a good half-mile for my body to acclimate to the pain. Initially there was an uncomfortable tingling sensation in my feet and legs, but eventually it all just went numb.

The trail leaving Foresthill would drop 2,500 feet to a river crossing in the valley. Worried that my quadriceps would crumble under this downhill pressure, I slowed considerably. Maybe I was capable of pushing harder, but the prospect of a complete breakdown was of utmost concern. After running 65 miles, you begin to lose touch with your body. The normal systems that monitor and transmit critical data to the brain begin to disintegrate and malfunction. The body starts playing tricks on the mind. Important physiological information is often communicated in sporadic pulses of pain that show up unannounced. Under normal circumstances, you would have at least some hint of the mounting tension, but after running 65 miles straight, your early warning signals become useless. One minute you're running along feeling satisfactory; the very next you're abruptly delivered a life-altering muscle cramp without warning.

The next two hours were run solo; I didn't see another human. As the late-afternoon sun turned the treetops gold, I felt alone in the wilderness. Vulnerable.

There were frequent mountain lion sightings around here, and earlier this year a runner had been attacked, dragged down a hill, and killed while training on the Western States trail.

I was in no condition to fend off a predator. My neck hurt, my shoulders hurt, my back hurt, my hips hurt, my knees hurt, my feet hurt, even the tip of my nose radiated pain. Every step hurt more than the last. At times like these you ask yourself the hard questions: How committed am I? How far am I willing to go?

There were only two people manning the next aid station at Ford's Bar. They had hiked in a considerable distance, carrying many of the supplies on their backs. Amazingly, they had hauled in a small camping table and had placed some chopped fruit and energy bars on it.

I sat in the dirt on the side of the trail. "Boy, am I glad to see you guys," I said in a scratchy voice.

One of the guys had long, straight black hair and chiseled features, like an old painting of a Native American. When the Indian spoke, his words were clear and deliberate.

"This is a difficult part of the journey," he said, finishing his sentence by gazing up to the sky. A hawk screeched off in the distance, and its cry resonated up the valley. It was like a scene from an old John Wayne Western, only with a runner lying in the dirt.

"Have you done this run before?" I asked.

He turned his gaze back down to me. "Oh, yes, my

friend." He nodded very slowly and went back to watching the sky.

"Do you know what mileage it is at this point?"

"This is mile seventy-three," the other guy said. "The river's five miles down the valley." The next checkpoint was at the Rucky Chucky River Crossing. "How are you feeling?"

"I was doing okay up to Foresthill, but I've entered a world of hurt since. The pain is getting intense," I said.

There was a long moment of silence, and then the Indian chief began to speak. "That is to be expected," he said, continuing to scan the sky. "Pain is the body's way of ridding itself of weakness."

In my semiconscious and half-delirious state, it took a few moments to register. Even when I made partial sense of his words, I wasn't entirely sure what to do with them. *Wait a minute,* I thought. *What was it that Coach McTavish had said?* "If it feels good, you're doing something wrong. It's supposed to hurt like hell." Perhaps I was doing something right here. Perhaps I was actually purging my body of weakness. Instead of trying to suppress it, maybe I should relish the pain, celebrate it. Maybe I like pain . . .

They peeled me up from the trail and, grudgingly, I readied myself to carry on. Shuffling out of the small area, the chief had one last pearl of wisdom, "You can do it."

I looked back at him. "Thanks," I said, "I'm certainly going to try."

It seemed the sun would not set today. Nearing 8:30 P.M., it was perfectly framed in the bed of the valley, and I was running directly toward it, squinting to protect my eyes.

Pary loved the sunset. She would stare out of our kitchen window, which overlooked the Pacific, and watch it, transfixed. Sometimes she would run and find me, "Quick . . . quick, we're going to miss it!" and we'd race for the binoculars trying to get the best view of the "green flash"—that elusive, magical moment when the sun temporarily appears green just before disappearing below the horizon. "That was a good one," she would say. "The best one yet."

Near the bottom of the valley, the trail ran parallel to the American River. Off in the distance, I could see a couple of runners making their way toward the river crossing in front of me. They looked to be about a mile away. My progress seemed slow and labored, so it surprised me when I caught up to them so quickly.

Behold, it was my two friends from the "special" military.

All along I had known they were somewhere ahead of me, but I hadn't expected to catch them, especially both of them at the same time. It's highly unusual for two runners to maintain the same pace for 75 miles.

As slowly as I was running, they were moving even more sluggishly. The shorter of the two was hunched over so severely that his chin rested on his chest. His muscular arms swayed randomly back and forth like a gorilla as he moved.

My initial thought was to blow right by them without saying anything, but that didn't seem like the decent thing to do. Instead, I pulled up alongside the pair and said hello. Surprisingly, they exchanged greetings this time and seemed almost happy to see me. The stout one was really suffering. It was clear he had been sick at least once; dried vomit covered his chin, and his legs were swollen and knotted. It appeared that there was blood coming out of his ear, though I tried not to stare for too long.

The taller guy looked entirely together—almost fresh, in fact. His eyes were clear and bright, and he still had a lot of spring in his stride. He looked like he could have been running much faster.

"I thought we might see you somewhere along the trail," he said.

That's funny, I thought, *I didn't even think you knew I existed.*

We kept motoring along together for a little while. The short one was doing everything in his power to keep up with us, but I could tell it was taking a whole lot out of him to hold a steady pace without stopping. At one point he kicked a big rock in the trail and let out a bellowing groan.

"Listen," his partner said, "why don't you keep powering along and we'll catch up with you later?"

"Ah, sure," I replied. "I'll see you guys in a little while, at the river crossing or something."

It seemed clear, though, that the way things were going, we probably wouldn't be seeing each other again in this race. The short one croaked, "Keep it tight, brother. You're lookin' solid."

With seventy-five miles of torture to whittle away the defenses, they were revealed to be good guys at the core.

The sun had fallen below the horizon when I pulled up behind another runner some 45 minutes later.

"Hey, what up?" he said, without looking back.

"Not much. Just trying to make it to the river."

"Yeah, me too," he puffed. "I've got some tightness in my groin and I started pissing blood a few miles back. I don't know what the hell's going wrong. Guess I shouldn't be complaining, though. You see that poor bastard behind us?"

"You mean those two guys? It's kind of strange they're running together."

"Yeah," he said, "those Rangers are pretty fucked up, ain't they?"

Now I was totally confused. "I'm not sure I follow," I said. "Are they in the Forest Service?"

"No, they ain't no *forest* rangers," he said. "They're Army Rangers."

The picture was becoming clearer now.

"They're trained not to leave their partner," he went

on, "so they do *everything* together. The guy who looks fresh won't leave his partner for nothin', even if it means dropping out of the race himself. They'll either finish the race together or drop out together. So if one of them goes down, they're both out. I used to train with an ex-Ranger. Those guys are pretty fuckin' psycho if you ask me." He burst into a wry cackle.

As psycho as I was beginning to think this guy was, he was pretty engaging, and the distraction of running with him served me well. We ran together for the next couple of miles and he kept up a constant chatter.

We parted company at the Rucky Chucky checkpoint, where he was rushed to the hospital with acute renal failure. I guess having blood in your urine isn't a good sign.

A volunteer escorted me from the checkpoint down to the river crossing. He carried a pitcher of water and kept filling my bottles, urging me to keep drinking even though the sun had gone down. Just before crossing the river, I asked him if he had any last bits of advice.

"Yeah," he said with a strange conviction. "Don't stop, come hell or high water. And it looks like you've got both in front of you."

The dark, icy-cold river came up over my waist as I struggled across, trying not to slip on the rocky bottom and get swept downstream. Through the turbulence, I carefully plodded, step by awkward step, clumsily fighting to remain balanced and upright in the swift current. As I reached the distant shore, drenched from my chest down, I found that a rope had been attached to a tree on the hillside above. I used it to hoist myself wearily up the muddy embankment.

On the far side of the river crossing was an aid station staffed with students and professors from the University of California School of Podiatry. Many of the athletes were in dire need of foot repair by this point. I sat in a rickety lounge chair, and a podiatry student immediately knelt in front of me.

"I think there's a clam shell or something in my left shoe," I told him.

He removed my shoe and sock and shook a lot of sand and small rocks out, but no clam shell. Reaching inside the sock, he pulled something out and flashed his penlight on it.

"Is it a shell?" I asked.

"Uh, no." He held the object up. "That," he grinned, "would be your big toenail."

I was mortified, then amused. *How could I lose a toenail without knowing?*

"It's okay," I said to him calmly. "I wasn't that attached to it anyway."

He laughed and asked if he could keep it. I guess that's the kind of trophy a podiatry student keeps around the dorm.

We decided not to mess a whole lot with my feet. There wasn't much that could be done, really. From this point forward, it was principally a matter of damage control.

The Rucky Chucky River Crossing

Darkness had taken over, so I strapped on a head-lamp and switched on my handheld flashlight. Twenty-two miles separated me from the finish line. I had successfully navigated the high water; now would come the hell.

The Rucky Chucky River Crossing
to Auburn Lakes Trail
Miles 78 to 85.2

People say the real race begins after crossing the river. My watch read 9:51 P.M., which was, miraculously, a full hour ahead of a projected twenty-four-hour finishing pace. As I started down the trail, a man recording check-out times enthusiastically informed me that I was in 20th place.

"Geez," I said with some surprise, "I'm just happy to be alive."

It's hard to judge distances when running at night, especially on narrow trails. Your world is confined to the reach of your flashlight beam, and beyond that is just darkness. Detecting the contour of the terrain becomes impossible at times, and you're left running on little more than instinct. The climb from the river stretched out for 2 miles, and then the trail became a narrow tunnel through tall, heavy brush that smelt of dampness and earth. The brush was so overgrown that I often hacked along with my arms. Through the constant buzzing of crickets and croaking frogs, I'd periodically hear louder noises crashing through the brush and hope it was just a deer and not a cougar or bear.

Running with just the power of my headlamp and flashlight, I was again feeling very isolated. Mostly I liked the solitude of long-distance trail running, but in this weakened state I longed for the camaraderie of another runner. There were no other athletes in sight, no checkpoints, not even a jet in the sky. Was I still on the right trail? Not only was my body on the brink of collapse, I was now becoming apprehensive, seriously questioning what the hell I was doing out here. There was something deep and primitive about the experience, no doubt, but right now I didn't want an encounter that meaningful. Enough punishment already . . . Uncle! I longed to be sitting at home in my easy chair, beer in one hand and remote in the other, surfing mindlessly through repeats of *Seinfeld* and *Baywatch*.

And then, to make matters worse, both my headlight and flashlight dimmed unaccountably. I carried extra batteries in my pack, so I stopped and changed them. But the lights for some reason remained dim. Could the new batteries be just as weak? Or was it the bulbs?

There was nothing to do but keep running. The trail before me was almost completely black. Branches and tree limbs appeared to jump out at me from nowhere. I could now barely detect the tip of my outstretched hand. And then, strangely, I began seeing outlines of green around everything, as though I were looking through night-vision goggles. The trail and foliage around me started to glow like a film negative. What was going on?

I looked up at the sky. There were no stars to be seen. No Milky Way, no Big Dipper. It was a cloudless night in the mountains—there should be a thousand twinkling stars. Yet all I saw was darkness.

That's when I knew I was going blind.

It's called nyctalopia, or night blindness. It can be caused by lowered blood pressure or exposure to bright light during the day. The body's capacity to produce a chemical compound called rhodopsin, or visual purple, which is necessary for the perception of objects in dim light, is temporarily impaired.

The blisters had been uncomfortable, the muscle spasms agonizing, but going blind really presented an obstacle. I could only see a foot or two in front of me. I walked very slowly with my flashlight held out in front. The Auburn Lakes aid station at mile 85 was relatively close, and voices, or music, resonated off in the distance. Even while I plodded along at this painfully slow rate, my muscles and joints radiated pain every time my foot hit the ground. I found myself pausing slightly after each step, and it took tremendous concentration to move forward in a straight line without wavering back and forth across the trail. Finally I decided to just sit down and gather myself. Moving at a snail's pace was demoralizing.

Sitting on the trailside, I had a sickening sense that my journey had come to an abrupt end. I was bruised and bloodied and in no shape to contend with the beating for another sixteen miles to the finish line. Plus, I couldn't see. Maybe I should just be thankful to have made it this far. I'd covered nearly 85 miles along one of the most extreme trails in the world, displaying strength and resolve along the way, breaking through one barrier after the next, a respectable accomplishment. Still, I wasn't satisfied.

Most dreams die a slow death. They're conceived in a moment of passion, with the prospect of endless possibility, but often languish and are not pursued with the same heartfelt intensity as when first born. Slowly, subtly, a dream becomes elusive and ephemeral. People who've let their own dreams die become pessimists and cynics. They feel that the time and devotion spent on chasing their dreams were wasted. The emotional scars last forever. "It can't be done," they'll say, when you describe your dream, "You'll never make it."

My dream was dying. I didn't want to give up, but I seemed powerless to do anything about it. My decision was to wait for the next runner and ask him to send back help from the Auburn Lakes aid station, which was probably less than a mile ahead. I lay down in the dirt to wait—and promptly nodded off.

I awoke in confusion, not being able to place my whereabouts for a second. I could only have dozed for a few minutes, but it must have been a very deep slumber and it left me in a daze. When I finally gathered my senses, I recognized something odd and beautiful: the sky was again filled with shining stars. My vision had partially come back.

Suddenly I was infused with a renewed sense of hope. If I could see, I could move forward, and if I could move forward, I could continue chasing my dream. It might be slow going, but it certainly beat being carried out on a stretcher.

I sat up and turned on my flashlight and headlamp. The light they put out appeared weak and diffused, but it would do. It would have to do; I wasn't stopping.

The first few steps were like running on legs of marble. Pain shot from my foot to my pelvis like lightning bolts. Limping onward, I could now clearly hear rock music nearby. The checkpoint had to be within half a mile.

Then my eyesight began dimming again; the miraculous reprieve had been short-lived.

The aid station was so close that I could now detect lyrics to the songs and clearly hear laughter echoing off the hills. I marched blindly onward. Then there were lights, but they cast a weird rainbow glow, perhaps some new effect of the night blindness. I shook my head to clear my vision, but the colors remained steadfast.

I plodded toward them . . . and discovered that the colors were real. Someone had stung hundreds of Christmas lights throughout the forest. Just to screw with me, I'm sure.

At the station I was guided into a chair. People were asking me questions. The music was a Stones song: *"When the whip comes downnn . . . yeah, when the whip comes down!"* Another fitting choice for the day's sound track. More questions were thrown at me out of the shadows.

"I'm all right, I suppose," I managed to tell them. "But I kind of had a meltdown a few miles back. I'm having a hard time seeing."

"Oh, that's okay," came an enthusiastic reply. "We can fix that . . . Hey, Bob, bring over that yellow tackle box with all the batteries in it. This guy's flashlight is going dead."

"No," I said. "It's not the batteries."

"That's okay, too," he chirped. "We got extra bulbs as well."

"It's not the batteries or the bulbs . . . it's me. Something's going wrong with my vision."

There were several gasps in the crowd, and the guy helping me sputtered, "Oh, Jesus!"

Now there was a buzz of people all around me. They turned down the music, and I could hear lots of whispering. Someone moved behind my chair and began massaging my shoulders and neck.

"You still look pretty good," that person said. "It's too bad about your eyes."

There was some rustling and footsteps, and one of the other volunteers spoke. He cleared his voice a couple of times like the beginning of a town hall meeting.

"Okay, here's what we're going to do. We'll set you up on one of the cots and get you comfortable so you can sleep. Then in the morning, we'll get you out on horseback . . . how does that sound?"

"Well . . . ," I said, hesitantly. "It sounds pretty good. Except for one minor detail—I'm going to keep running."

A murmur buzzed through the crowd.

"But how you going to do that?" someone asked. "You can't see."

"Good question," I replied. "But I can't be concerned with details at this point."

It was a joke, but no one seemed to find it funny.

Somebody brought over a plate of brownies. Biting into one, I discovered that they were laced with espresso beans.

"Wow," I said, grinning. "That's definitely going to put some life back in me."

The small crowd got a kick out of my attempt at humor, but I think they were mostly laughing at the mess I was making with the brownies.

In a few minutes, the effects of the caffeine and sugar took hold. The jolt hit me like a mild electrical shock. I'd never eaten whole espresso beans before, and the experience was marvelous. Almost instantaneously I was wired.

Oddly, the lift helped my vision, and I could now distinctly make out the individual colors of each light. *Why Christmas lights?* I wondered. This whole scene was very bizarre, almost like I'd entered an *Alice in Wonderland* story. Perhaps there was more in those brownies than just caffeine. Or perhaps the nineteen hours of continuous running had altered my brain chemistry in some unusual way. Whatever might be going on, the net effect was vitalizing; my senses were firing.

As I wolfed down another brownie in preparation for departure, someone asked, "Are you sure you know what you're doing?"

"No," I replied. "I have absolutely no idea what I'm doing. In fact, I'm not even sure where I'm at right now."

That drew plenty of laughs, but it wasn't intended as a joke. I really had no idea what I was doing; this was entirely uncharted territory for me. At least I now had *hope,* which is more than what I'd had an hour ago.

"You've got balls, buddy," a volunteer said as I headed off into the night. "Good luck."

Chapter 10

Forever Changed

> *Bid me run, and I will strive with*
> *things impossible.*
>
> —Shakespeare, *Julius Caesar*

Auburn Lakes to Robie Point
Midnight, June 26, 1994

The trail weaved back into thick foliage, with rocks and branches strewn across the path, but the lift from those magic brownies carried me along pleasantly. My step was more nimble and lighter than it had been. Clearly I was tapping into a reserve that I might not have adequate capital to cover in the not-too-distant future. Surely it wasn't normal to feel so energetic 87 miles into a run. This had to be deficit spending.

Medical analysis of blood samples taken from previous Western States participants has shown that some muscle destruction occurs in all runners. The harder one pushes, the deeper one digs, the more extensive the damage can be. Complete recovery usually takes several months, but I was certain it would take much longer in my case. In fact, the way I was pushing, it was questionable if I'd be walking again this year.

The normally sleepy Auburn Faith Community Hospital was going to be a busy place tonight. I'd overheard that a crowd of runners had already filled the emergency room. Most were just in need of intravenous electrolytes and glucose, but there was the occasional laceration and a few broken bones. The ER was not the place I wanted my journey to end.

Halfway to the next and final checkpoint at mile 94, my senses were preternaturally acute. An owl hooted off in the distance, and the sound was crisp and clear, as though it were only inches from my ear. A warm gust of air rippled across the front of my jersey, and the pattern of ebb and flow seemed entirely predictable, almost visible. This was more than just a "runner's high." This was an out-of-body experience, more potent than anything I'd encountered before.

Unfortunately, the levity was fleeting. The high dissipated more quickly than I would have liked, and the last mile to the checkpoint was more about fortitude than running. A thick cloud of dust trailed behind me as I shuffled in, now barely able to lift my feet enough to clear the ground. The crash of the earlier buzz had left me in a corresponding deep low. I declined a chair, knowing that I would instantly tighten if I stopped.

From this last checkpoint, the finish line was just six miles to the east. Nothing more than a standard 10K, something I could usually do easily. The remaining terrain was flat compared to what I'd covered, but there was still one wicked 900-foot ascent to contend with, and it came at the very end of the course. Imagine scaling three Heartbreak Hills after having run ninety-seven miles through the mountains. This race was remorseless, bordering on psychotic. My body was being pushed to the limits of physical endurance—that much I could understand—but my mind was being played with in surreptitious ways. Would the trail ever end? Or would I eventually reach the edge of the earth and fall off into the abyss?

With my water bottles refilled, I began agonizingly making my way toward the exit. As I did, the small crowd clapped and hooted, whistled and rang bells. It was after midnight, and for these people to be out here in the middle of nowhere showing such spirit gave me goose bumps. My eyes watered with hope.

Ten minutes down the trail, I wished I'd been pulled from the event. Those tears of euphoria were replaced by tears of excruciating pain. The transition from high to low had happened so quickly that even covering a hundred feet—let alone six miles—was vexing. My quadriceps tightened further with each tender step. I was afraid to keep running for fear of cramping . . . but also afraid to stop for fear of cramping; so I chose a median, and began walking.

The trail emerged from the thickets into a vast, grassy meadow. There was a slight breeze blowing across the expanse, and a landscape of long supple reeds swayed gently in the wafts of warm air. Light-colored soil made up the path, and the trail succinctly dissected the grassy span for as far as the cast of my lights could reach. In the pale moonlight, I could detect no end to the meadow as I walked along.

Actually, it was a pleasant stroll . . . until the first mosquito stung my neck. Then another buzzed in my ear. Then one struck my leg. A swarm of the little bloodsuckers surrounded my torso. Two dozen more circled overhead.

I raced down the trail, screaming. I could only sprint a short distance before my legs shrieked in agony and I was forced to slow; and then the tiny savages caught up with me again, and I forced myself to strike back out on a run. We continued this cat-and-mouse game across the meadow and up a gradual incline, where the warmer, drier air and brisker breeze abated the nuisance.

My heart raced and perspiration dripped down my face. I'd already drunk one of my water bottles dry, and I needed to conserve the other for farther up the trail. There were no more aid stations left. But I was overheating and risked dehydration if I didn't keep drinking. So I gulped from the second bottle, depleting my remaining supply.

Coming over a minor embankment, I sensed movement up ahead by the side of the trail. I flashed my light at it. When a light flashed back at me, I knew it must be another runner, or one very smart bear.

It turned out to be a pacer, actually; the runner was lying flat on his back.

"I'm letting him nap a little while," the pacer explained. "He's been puking for about the last ten miles and he was starting to drift off, so it seemed like a good time to rest."

I looked down at the runner with my headlamp. He was sleeping on the ground, completely stiff, and his face appeared jaundiced.

"Are you staying with him all the way to the finish?"

"If we can get that far," he said. "You know what DNF stands for, don't you?"

"Yeah," I replied. "I've been trying to repress those words for the past ninety-five miles."

"At this point in the race," he went on, "it stands for 'Did Nothing Fatal.' "

We both knew what he meant. The race isn't over until you cross the finish line. People have been forced to quit with less than a mile left, for reasons that weren't always voluntary.

"You see that light up there?" he said, pointing off into the distance.

"Yes, I see it."

"That's Robie Point. That's where we need to go."

Robie Point is where the Western States trail leaves

the wilderness for the paved city streets of Auburn. From Robie Point it's just over a mile to the finish line on the Placer High School track. That light at Robie Point was faint and fleeting and well off in the distance.

"Where's your pacer?" he asked.

"Big mistake—I haven't got one."

"Whew," he said. "You don't want to be out here all alone, it gets kind of hairy."

"I know. It's my first States and I didn't really understand what I was getting into."

"Man, if it's your first time, you're killing it! To make it this far in this amount of time is phenomenal."

Now, if I could just live to tell the story, it would be all the better.

I thanked him and pressed on. The path entered a twisting succession of zigzag turns. Although the cornering was tricky as I ran along, the pitch remained surprisingly flat and even. Suddenly I detected a substantial void between the slope that I was on and the rise of the adjacent hill. It wasn't possible to fly between the two, so there was probably going to be an abrupt topological change in the not-too-distant future.

And soon enough, the trail literally dropped out from under my feet. I lurched forward, with no surface beneath me, and began free-falling. When my foot finally contacted the ground, the speed was too much to remain upright. I tripped, fell, and wheeled down the slope like a barrel, eventually crashing into a sturdy shrub.

I lay there on my back gazing up at the sky while the world whirled round and round. Afraid to move, I remained motionless.

When my head finally stopped spinning, I inched myself up. I'd been deposited on a small ledge, with a steep drop below me. Thank god that shrub had arrested my fall—who knows where I might have ended-up otherwise?

The embankment that I'd tumbled down was composed of loose sandstone; it wasn't going to be easy getting back up. After collecting my senses, I slowly rose, took a deep breath, and began a calculated charge up the hillside. The footing was sandy, my feet sank as I dug in, but I desperately clawed my way to the top.

Debris filled both my shoes. *Screw it, no need to empty them out.* My feet were toast anyway. Best just to keep moving forward.

Rattled by the fall, I labored down the trail with reserve, watching for other unmarked drop-offs. The trail wove confusingly through tall shrubs for a while and then stopped abruptly at a sheer rock wall.

Clearly they didn't expect for us to free-climb a vertical rock face, did they? I searched for a way around the obstruction, thinking that perhaps the trail was hidden from view. But blocking all potential exit routes were thick and impenetrable bushes.

Then it occurred to me: this was not the Western States trail at all. I was lost. Time to make a U-turn.

Backtracking was deflating. I've made my share of

mistakes over the years, but this was an exceptionally costly blunder, wreaking havoc on my psyche. I'd fallen down a hill and then taken a costly detour. How much worse could it possibly get?

The answer, unfortunately, was "much."

The final climb to Robie Point was hellacious. My remaining water was consumed early in the ascent, leaving me dry. I marched wearily upward, stumbling frequently. My hands were cut, and my arms and legs were bruised and scraped.

After I'd contended with this beastly climb for about as long as my body could hold up, the lights of Robie Point finally came into view. I was coated in dirt and drooling on myself as I covered the last few feet of approach. My eyes were nearly shut; all I could see was the ground a few feet in front of me.

A man stood there with a record log. When he saw me, he dropped the clipboard and ran over to help. I crumpled into his outstretched arms, and he slowly lowered my body to the ground. He was talking to me, almost yelling, but I was fading in and out and couldn't comprehend a word.

Then another face appeared above me. It was oddly familiar.

"Dad?"

"My God, son," he replied gravely. "What's happened to you?"

He knelt down beside me and took my head in his hands. There were tears streaming down his cheeks. He cradled my body gently, as though trying to protect any last bits of life that were still left inside.

"Where's Mom?" I whispered. "I don't want her to see me like this."

My father choked back tears. "Don't worry, son. She's waiting at the finish line."

"Dad," I said weakly, "I'm not sure what to do at this point. I can barely move."

"Son," he said resolutely, "if you can't run, then walk. And if you can't walk, then crawl. Do what you have to do. Just keep moving forward and never, ever give up."

He closed his eyes and held me tightly. I reached up and put my hand on his shoulder. "I will, Dad," I muttered. "I won't give up."

He loosened his hold and I rolled onto my stomach. I got my arms and legs in place and then simply followed his instructions: I began crawling up the road. I could hear Dad trying to control his crying as I dragged my body off into the distance.

Robie Point to Oblivion
Mile 99 and Beyond

The course was now on paved city streets, but it was still pitch-dark. There were no lampposts along this back-country road on the outskirts of town. No side-walks, either, so I crawled up the middle of the dark road. I rose to my feet and shuffled when capable, but mostly I crawled. Slower and slower I progressed, until my legs were nearly useless and I inched forward using primarily my arms.

The finish was less than a mile away, but it was bullheaded ambition to continue onward in this manner. I would never make it at this rate, the odds were impossible. Still, nothing was going to stop me.

Not even the car that came barreling down the road at me.

I stopped crawling and waved my flashlight at it. Eventually the driver slammed on the brakes, then pulled up beside me. A man and woman leaped out.

"Are you all right?!"

I was flat on my stomach in the road. Slanting my head sideways, I muttered, "Never felt better."

"Oh, thank God," the woman cried. "We thought you got hit by a car."

"Nah," I groaned. "I just look that way."

I contorted myself into a sitting position and explained what was going on. They offered to help, but there really wasn't much they could do. The finish line was so close, but it just as well could have been on a different continent. Destroyed, I reclined on the warm asphalt in front of them, thoroughly defeated.

But when my back hit the ground, a strange phenomenon began: my mind started to replay the events of the day. And through all the pain and despair I'd experienced over the past ninety-nine miles, the memories that came flooding in were good ones of all the people who had helped me along the path. Jim the "foot-repair man." Nate the water guy at Last Chance. The lady who baked magic brownies. My sister, who inspired me in life, and whose spirit inspired me to this day. The final scene that played through my mind was that of the Indian chief at the Ford's Bar aid station and the last words he had said to me: "You can do it."

It hit me as if I'd awoken from a dream, only to realize that I wasn't dreaming at all. I turned to the couple standing by their car and defiantly proclaimed, "I can."

They both stared at me. With even more resilience in my voice I repeated, "I can!"

They blinked at me, but the husband played along.

"Yes," he bellowed. "Yes, you can!"

I jumped to my feet and started shaking my arms and legs wildly. I swung my head around, letting out an animal-like growl. And then I took off, dashing up the road, shouting, "I can! I can!"

The initial few steps were agonizing, but it's not like the hurt came as some big surprise. I knew what to expect by this point. Though it hurt like never before, I no longer just numbly accepted the pain for what it was. Now I went after it, sought it out, hunted it down. The pain radiated from every cell in my body, and my response was to push even harder. The tables were turned. *To hell with the pain: Bring it on!*

I don't know precisely when I broke through the last wall, but it was sometime during this final melee. The initial breakthroughs along the way had all been physical, about trying to deal with exhaustion and bodily fatigue. After mile 50, they had been battles of the mind. But this last breakthrough was much more hallowed, and it touched me on a deeper level than the others, more like an awakening.

It struck me in the space of a few steps that my past as I knew it had suddenly ceased to exist. Nothing would ever be the same to me from this point on. I'd been profoundly transformed by this journey, in ways I had yet to understand. This person who was staggering and crawling and persisting at mile 99 was a different being than the guy who had started the race just yesterday morning. I was more capable than I imagined, better than I ever thought I could be. This realization was like stepping into another dimension.

Covering 100 miles on foot was more than a lesson in survival, it was an education on the grace of living. Running is a solo sport, but it was no longer about me anymore; I became almost irrelevant. My struggles were not about a single runner trying to finish this unfathomable challenge but about the greater ability of a human being to persevere against insurmountable odds. The many supporters who'd provided encouragement and strength along the way didn't really care about me per se—hell, they didn't even know who I was. What they cared about was that a person had taken the time to train, and sacrifice, and dedicate himself wholeheartedly to the pursuit of a dream. It was a powerful message; I was just the host. And proud to be. Upholding my end of the commitment meant crossing the finish line, and I was now going to make damn sure that happened. For all of us.

I ran freely now, paying little attention to the ground in front of me or the pain. It's funny how a dream that has almost been lost can come back to life with such power. Its rebirth infuses you with a vitality that's both playful and shockingly resolute. Suddenly obstacles cease to exist. The only thing that matters is making that dream come true.

That final half-mile into the Placer High stadium was run as though nothing else mattered. My shoes were falling off, my toes were bloodied, my shirt dangled by threads—all irrelevant. What mattered was making it to the finish line.

Big tears streamed down my cheeks as I entered the stadium to run that final lap around the track. I began laughing and crying at the same time as I ran those last few steps. It was just after 2:00 A.M. and the stadium was nearly empty, except for a few diehards that fed off this sort of raw energy. They were standing on their seats, clapping and cheering as I ran, proudly crying, across the finish line. If pure emotion and passion are what these people wanted to see, they had come to the right place.

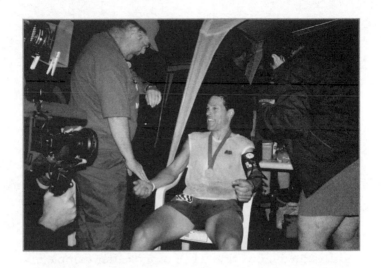

Medical check at the Western States finish

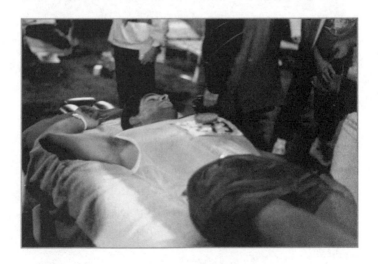

Laid out at the Western States finish

The emotion got the better of me as well. That announcer at the start of the race had been right: I was forever changed by the Western States experience. Everything took on new meaning. My demeanor grew more carefree, as if the important things in life had become clearer. My outlook became more expansive; my shortcomings less significant. Others were treated with greater compassion, increased tolerance, broader humility.

I liked the transformation this race brought about, and I wanted more. Scarcely a month after completing the event, I found myself lusting for the next challenge. My official finishing time was twenty-one hours, one minute, and fourteen seconds, and I had come in 15th place overall. Respectable for a rookie, given that this was one of the most elite ultra-endurance running fields on earth. Not that I cared much about my placing. Passion had fueled my progress, and I hungered for more.

It was optimistic to think that I could run farther than 100 miles, especially under such demanding conditions, but I yearned to test the limits of human endurance and stretch the limits of self. I was listening to my heart, finding my place in the world. If it could be done, I wanted to do it. Because I needed to know how far I could go.

Part Two

Chapter 11

Badwater

Running with the devil . . .

—Van Halen

Death Valley
July 26, 1995

There is a temperature at which bread begins to toast. I'm not exactly sure what that temperature is— but I can say from experience that running in such heat is not advisable.

After I'd successfully completed the Western States 100-Mile Endurance Run, life became a little more vibrant. There was a certain spring in my stride, a newfound levity in my disposition. Even if most people I interacted with had no idea of what I'd done, I knew. That was all that mattered. The greatest rewards of high achievement, I had come to believe, were intrinsic.

Beyond Western States, I didn't know of any physical challenge more demanding. That is, until I read a short piece in the *Los Angeles Times* about an obscure footrace across Death Valley in the middle of summer.

Badwater is the lowest point in the Western Hemisphere, smack in the middle of Death Valley, at the southeastern end of California, 282 feet below sea level. Summertime temperatures can exceed 130 degrees Fahrenheit, and the asphalt can get better than 200 degrees. Not your ideal place for a jog.

But the summer after I completed the Western States, I found myself standing at the starting line of the Badwater Ultramarathon, drenched in perspiration, shaking with anticipation, waiting for the race to begin.

Twenty-four of us were about to embark on what is called *The World's Toughest Footrace*—a 135-mile trek across Death Valley to Mount Whitney, the highest peak in the contiguous United States. While the Western States 100-Mile Endurance Run had been grueling, Badwater is widely considered the ultimate test of endurance and human resolve. Or just plain insanity. It can go either way.

Athletes have traveled from across the globe to take on Badwater. The fittest of the fit have come here to push the body to unthinkable limits in hopes of reaching the finish within the official cutoff time of sixty hours. Unlike Western States, Badwater is a road race held entirely on paved highway. But there are still plenty of hills to contend with along the route, even before the road begins its twisted ascent up Mount Whitney.

Scanning the starting line, what I saw was the most elite squadron of extreme endurance athletes on the face of the earth. They were clad in white desert suits, muscles taut underneath, preparing to embark on the ultimate physical challenge. And there I stood among them, heart pounding in the sweltering heat, ready to rumble.

I'd spent the entire year training for Badwater, adapting my routine in preparation for the harsh conditions by running in a wool sweater and ski parka, attempting to simulate the desert heat. In talking with some of the other competitors around the starting line, it sounded like my training might have been light. Many of them trained inside a sauna.

With a chorus of hoots and primordial screams from the racers and support crew (I didn't see a single spectator in the crowd), the race began. The heat was like nothing I had ever encountered before, completely otherworldly. Undulating waves of solar radiation rose from the pavement in massive sheets as we made our way down the long, straight, featureless highway. A runner in the distance quickly became engulfed by the mirage that distorted everything on the horizon.

Because the route we followed was entirely along the roadside, I'd decided to rent a motor home as a crew vehicle. Bad choice. As we'd crossed the desert in it on the way to the starting line, the alternator had fried, leaving my family and newly arrived daughter, Alexandria, stranded in a 125-degree immobile motor home. It was a risky decision bringing Alexandria, at six months old, to this event. Most guidebooks advised not taking children to Death Valley in the summer months. But I didn't want to leave her. Luckily I had Julie, my folks, and my uncle George along for support.

Fearing for Alexandria's safety, and ours as well, we hastily abandoned the broken-down RV and fled for shelter, leaving most of my running gear, food, and supplies inside.

Thankfully a park ranger found us shortly after we'd left the vehicle on the roadside, and he drove us to shelter. With the RV cooked, Julie, my mother, and Alexandria got a ride with the ranger back to a hotel near the end of the race in a little town called Lone Pine. Uncle George went with them and picked up his Mazda sedan that he'd left in town when we met. I would now be supported during the race not by my entire family in a motor home, but by a skeleton crew consisting of my father and uncle in a compact car. We had only salvaged one small cooler from the RV, and we had very little ice. It was far from ideal, but out in Death Valley you take what you can.

The ordeal on the way to the start had been unsettling, but I tried not to let it break my composure. Every inch of my flesh was covered with a white UV protective suit— like a running mummy—to prevent the sun from searing my skin. I needed to focus on staying cool, on not over-

Running down the white line on the
highway to hell

heating inside the suit. There wasn't a tree in sight, not
even so much as a rock to crawl under for shade.

The asphalt quickly grew so hot that it literally melted
my first pair of running shoes within an hour. I didn't
see it coming, the soles just disintegrated. I switched to
a second pair. Watching some of the other competitors,
I learned to run down the white line that edged the
roadside, which reflected enough heat to keep this new
pair from melting, at least for the time being.

Even running down the white line, the inferno radiating off the road surface was like a blast furnace. Within twelve miles, my feet developed blisters. By 15 miles, blisters formed on top of my blisters. We stopped and cut huge swaths out of my shoes, reducing them to makeshift sandals. It helped a little.

We'd been advised to carry a plant mister to help me stay cool, and we'd brought one. But without ice, the mister was useless. As hard as I sprayed, most of the mist evaporated as it came out of the nozzle and never reached my body.

Earlier this year, a European tourist had roasted to death in the mudflats beside the road. Apparently, he had walked out to take some pictures. The coroner's report noted that the corpse's feet were severely disfigured. Poor bastard had stepped through the narrow surface crust into a layer of molten-hot mud. Trapped by the ankles, he'd literally baked to death. He, too, had been carrying a water mister—a lot of good that did him. . . .

Furnace Creek is the first remote outpost along the course, seventeen miles from the start. There is a small service station—which was closed—and a hotel, and lots of scorching red sand blowing across the road. To conserve our limited supplies, I guzzled from the gas-station hose before noticing a small placard next to the spigot: NON-POTABLE WATER.

Badwater.

The vomiting started at mile 30. Severe dehydration and cramping followed. I was less than a quarter of the way into it, and already things were going haywire.

My friend Tom Servais hosing me down at Badwater

"How about trying some food?" my dad asked from the Mazda window.

"Sure, I'll try anything."

He lowered the window and handed me a peanut butter and jelly sandwich. I ran with the sandwich for perhaps a hundred yards, trying to stave off the nausea enough to take a bite. When I finally chomped into it, I found that the bread was toasted. *That's strange,* I thought to myself, *Why would we bring a toaster to Death Valley?* Then it occurred to me: I was *running* in a toaster.

It was 1:00 A.M. as we made our way into Stovepipe Wells, 42 miles from the starting point of this godforsaken race. The road was dark and silent as I ran, except for the whistle of the wind howling across the barren expanse of desert and the periodic tumbleweed bouncing along the way. It was pitch-black when we arrived—the middle of the night—and the temperature was 112 degrees. Birds had fallen from the sky earlier in the day.

Stovepipe Wells has a single hotel, with a small pool. I ran straight to it and jumped in. Unfortunately, the water was as warm as a Jacuzzi. As I climbed out, another runner ambled up to the pool. He was dry-heaving continually, and, under the pale-yellow glow of the naked bulb illuminating the area, I could see him lurching uncontrollably. He stepped feetfirst into the pool without removing any of his running gear, shoes included. He was still dry-heaving when he clambered back out, dripping wet. He passed his crew in a daze.

"Did it help?" one of them asked.

He shook his head and staggered past them, straight into the hotel. That was the last we saw of him. Game over.

Exiting Stovepipe Wells, I was hallucinating vividly as I trotted along. The farther I progressed, the more delirious I became. At one point an old miner appeared in the road ahead of me, gold-dust pan in hand. *"Water,"* he croaked. Feeling sorry for him, I filled his pan from my bottle. It was only when the water splashed and steamed on the road that I realized he was a hallucination. Or a ghost.

Then came hallucinations of rattlesnakes on the road. "Look out!" my dad and uncle screamed, flashing the headlights and honking. The snakes were real.

Besides the rattlesnakes, there were scorpions and big tarantulas to watch out for on the dark road. My vision wasn't very focused, and my mind was in a haze. I plodded along recklessly, unable to remain mentally attentive. My guard was down at a time I needed to tread cautiously.

At four in the morning, along with the vomiting came severe diarrhea. My stride was so shaky that I could barely make it to the shoulder of the road to yank down my shorts and expel wretchedly from both ends simultaneously. The next remote outpost, Panamint Springs, was at mile 72. I needed to get there soon, if only for a roll of toilet paper. We had run out long ago.

My dad and uncle were with me straight through the night. They would pull the car some two miles up the road—looking for critters—and then would wait for me to saunter by, always ready to help. Although I'd stopped eating and drinking long ago, for fear of ejecting the products, they kept up the support all the way through.

The toughest footrace on earth was kicking my ass. The official finish at road-end on the side of Mount Whitney was still 63 miles away, and I had no intentions of stopping there. With my newfound spirited determination, I wanted to make an extreme endurance event even more extreme by blasting through the finish line and running eleven additional miles up the trail to the summit.

Call me a masochist. Plenty of people were starting to. I was thinking that myself as I staggered into Panamint Springs, hunched over like an ape. My head was spinning and I saw stars, though it was now daylight. Someone decided I needed fruit and stuffed a piece of warm, limp cantaloupe in my mouth. I threw it up immediately.

"Is he all right?" I heard a man ask my crew. It was Ben Jones, M.D., the local doctor, surgeon, obstetrician, pediatrician, psychiatrist (lord knows they need one out here), and mayor of Badwater.

"We're not sure," my dad answered.

"Would he like to use my ice bath?"

Behind his car, Dr. Jones was towing a coffin on wheels filled with ice water.

I shook my head. There was no way in hell I was crawling into a coffin, even for an icy cold bath. The prospect of ending up in one for good seemed all too real.

I could dimly make out the doctor consulting with my dad and uncle. They sounded like a bad transistor radio, complete with static and irregular volume. I looked up; the sun appeared to be pouring down in a molten red mist that swirled around the distant dunes and then weirdly evaporated back up into the sky. I took a step forward, veered sideways, took another wobbly half-step, and collapsed in a heap on the burning ground. . . .

When I awoke, the hotel sheets had been removed from the bed, and I was lying naked in a puddle of sweat.

"Where am I?" I mumbled. "Dad? Uncle George?"

"Would you like a towel?" my wife asked softly.

I squinted up at her face. "What are you doing here? Where are we?"

"The race is over, honey. You're at a hotel in Lone Pine."

"But I didn't finish, did I? How did I get here?"

"You were driven here. You passed out."

"No!" I croaked. "Why did they take me away?"

"Let's see: you were severely dehydrated, vomiting, slurring your words, and on the verge of heatstroke."

"So?"

"So when you passed out, they thought enough was enough."

"But I was only halfway done."

"It sounds like you were all the way done."

"I can't believe they carted me away like that."

"Would you like me to take you back out there?" she volunteered.

The idea of heading back into that inferno triggered an impulse of nausea. I sat up, wincing. I could see circular pus stains discoloring the sheets where my blisters had oozed a yellowy discharge from the abscesses covering both heels.

"I failed. I'm a failure."

"You did not fail, and you are certainly not a failure," Julie said firmly. "You ran seventy-two miles without being able to keep anything in your system. How much farther are you willing to go?"

To Julie, the bad luck encountered out in the desert

was just something to be taken in stride, a bump in the road, not the end of the road. There would be other races to run.

Julie was rational. I wasn't. To me, it was complete, incomprehensible devastation not to finish Badwater. It didn't occur to me that this distorted overreaction possibly came from the same internal force that drove me to run great distances and allowed me to endure unfathomable amounts of pain. Most people would let it go at a point. Win some, lose some. But to me, failure was terminal. In my way of looking at things, it was more honorable to die trying than to give up. Thank God I'd passed out back there; who knows what I might have done to myself otherwise.

Much of my bullheadedness, I knew, came as a result of losing my sister. After Pary's untimely death, life became more real. People can say things to you like, "You never know when your number's going to come up," but it doesn't really mean much until you have someone you love taken away from you unexpectedly. From that day on, my delusions of immortality ended. Every minute now mattered. There were no second chances with life; you really *didn't* know when your number would come up. Failure was insufferable to me. I had no time to waste failing.

"Let's pack it up," I said glumly. "We're a long way from home."

I felt awful. The list of those I'd disappointed was long. Not only had I let down everyone who had supported me along the way, I had put my family in harm's way and had nothing to show for this imprudence but a broken heart and shin splints. Worst of all, I had failed my sister, my greatest inspiration.

Had I let myself down? The pain ran much deeper than that. I wasn't even worthy of consideration. I didn't matter. I was nothing more than a loathsome creature undeserving of the least bit of sympathy. Mere self-pity was three rungs above the dark hole where I resided. My honor was shattered.

During the long drive home with my family, there was ample time to reflect on the lessons from Badwater, and I eased up on myself. Yes, I had failed—but it had actually been a spectacular failure, gloriously disintegrating every aspect of my body and soul until I literally fell over in the dirt. In the words of Theodore Roosevelt:

> The credit belongs to the man who is actually in the arena, whose face is marred by dust and sweat and blood; who strives valiantly; who errs, who comes short again and again, because there is no effort without error and shortcoming; but who does actually strive to do the deeds; who knows great enthusiasms, the great devotions; who spends himself in a worthy cause; who at the best knows in the end the triumph of high achievement, and who at the worst, if he fails, at least fails while daring greatly, so that his place shall never be with those cold and timid souls who neither know victory nor defeat.

Boy, did I know defeat. There was really no defeat more devastating than running oneself into the ground short of the finish line. I'd gone head to head with the world's toughest footrace, and lost. Despite my greatest efforts, Badwater had pounded me into submission.

It was pure, unadulterated defeat. But what I came to realize on the drive home was that I'd loved every second of it.

Alive and back home after Badwater
with Julie and Alexandria

Chapter 12

Frozen Stiff

*Only those who will risk going too far can
possibly find out how far they can go.*

—T. S. Eliot

*The South Pole
January 2002*

After failing at Badwater in 1995, I went back the
next summer to seek redemption. This time around I
trained even harder, bracing my body for the punishment I knew it would encounter along the way. The
pounding was no less severe than in the first attempt,
but my body and will surmounted the abuse this time,
and I made it. However, succeeding at Badwater didn't
satiate my hunger for adventure; it fed it.

I embarked on a search-and-enjoy mission, throwing
myself at any extreme endurance test that could be de-

vised. If it required strength, stamina, and a lack of better judgment, I was game. I scaled Yosemite's infamous Half Dome, swam across the San Francisco Bay, did triathlons, adventure races, and twenty-four-hour mountain-bike rides. I climbed mountains, snowboarded down mountains, and surfed the massive liquid mountains off Northern California, Maui, Fiji, and Tahiti. And I continued to run like a wildman: running, to me, remained the purest form of athletic expression. It was the simplest, least encumbered sport there was, and the definitive measurement of raw stamina.

Photo courtesy of Tom Servais

Another favorite sport, windsurfing

Over the course of the decade, I managed to amass nine more Western States Silver Buckles. Scattered about the house were now dozens of medals, plaques, and trophies, and there was a massive steel sculpture for bagging the coveted Outdoor World Championships, a week-long, multi-sport event that included trail running, mountain biking, windsurfing, climbing, and a triathlon. Of course it's cool to have mementos like these, but I didn't have them on display in the living room or haul them out for family get-togethers or cocktail parties. Some were in closets, others were buried in drawers beneath piles of running socks, and most were in boxes in the garage. It wasn't acclaim I craved, but adventures that involved out-of-body experiences, intense pain, nights without sleep, and a supreme sense of accomplishment.

Hardly a month would pass when I didn't enter a 100-mile, 100-kilometer, or at the very least a 50-mile race. When there wasn't an organized ultra-endurance race happening, I'd do marathons just as training runs. My body reached a level of fitness that defied all sensible limitations. On the weekends, I could easily run all night and spend all day playing with Alexandria and our newly arrived son Nicholas, and I did so regularly. During the week, I trained early in the morning and late at night, because I worked nine-to-five. My resting heart rate hovered in the 30s, about the same as Lance Armstrong's.

As fewer and fewer organized events offered the kind of challenge I was after, I improvised by running from our house to the starting line, timing my arrival to coincide with the gun going off. Once I ran from our house in San Francisco across the Golden Gate Bridge to the start of the Miwok 100K in the Marin Headlands, a distance of about thirteen miles, and managed to finish the race a respectable 4th overall, winning my age division, among an elite field of racers. Then I went windsurfing.

No challenge was grand enough. Until a renowned mountaineering expedition leader, Doug Stoup, proposed running a marathon to the South Pole.

Antarctica, after all, is as low as you can go. The mercilessly cold climate and shifting frozen terrain there set the standard by which all other extreme adventures must be measured. How fitting that Ernest Shackleton's 1914 to 1916 expedition to be the first to cross Antarctica, one of the greatest survival stories of all time, was in a ship called *Endurance*. It's also sobering to remember that the Antarctic ice floes crushed and sank the legendary vessel before it got very far. Antarctica is the place where the strongest and bravest men pit themselves against the most pitilessly extreme elements on the planet, testing every shred of their perseverance and stamina just to stay alive. And the Shackleton drama played out along the more temperate fringes of the continent.

What may have been the most epic race of all time, a contest to reach the South Pole, took place deeper on the continent, at the geographic bottom of the earth—the polar plateau—where conditions are far more extreme. In 1911, Roald Amundsen, a Norwegian, and Robert Scott, an Englishman, vied for the glory and honor of leading the first expedition to reach the South Pole. Amundsen got there first, then made it out before the harshest weather hit. Scott arrived a scant month behind him . . . and never returned. The members of his ill-fated expedition would later be discovered frozen solid. The lowest temperature ever recorded on the planet was not far from where their trip ended. It reached an astounding –128.6 degrees Fahrenheit.

Yes, the South Pole would be a fine place to run a marathon. There was only one problem: nobody knew if it was possible.

Photo courtesy of Kris Erickson

Base camp, Antarctica

Five other athletes and I decided to take up the challenge. We would be the first group in history to attempt running a marathon to the South Pole. People had skied and used snowshoes to get to the bottom of the earth, but no one had ever run there. We would be the guinea pigs, the experimental crash-test dummies. To us endurance types, this was naturally very alluring.

There were plenty that doubted it could be done, and conventional wisdom said it would be impossible to run a marathon to the South Pole. But Doug Stoup didn't live by conventional wisdom. He found three experienced mountaineering guides and one medical doctor willing to accompany us.

My flight to the southern tip of Chile, where I met my fellow travelers—the athletes, the guides, and the doctor—took twenty-one hours. Then we all boarded a windowless Ilyushin cargo jet for the final leg of the journey. It was gloomy and stark in the jet's hold, with exposed wiring that snaked everywhere, and the ceaseless roar of the engines was deafening. The small Russian crew moved around casually, as though they were used to it. Five teeth-rattling hours later, we made our descent into Patriot Hills, Antarctica: Base Camp.

Patriot Hills lies more than a thousand miles into the frozen heart of the Antarctic, yet it's still some 600 miles from the South Pole. A desolate little outpost of fluttering tents and plastic waste barrels, it hunkers between the jagged white peaks of the Ellsworth Mountains to the south and a vast, open snow-plain to the north. It was below zero when we arrived, and gusting icy winds peppered the group as we staggered out of the jet's hold.

Those severe blasts of frigid air are an almost constant condition at Patriot Hills. The outpost huddles defense-less and vulnerable in the direct path of the savage glacial airstream (officially known as "katabatic" winds) that roars remorselessly down from the polar plateau. The winds originate from the intense high-pressure cell that's permanently clamped over the South Pole. It's the steep drop of altitude and pressure between the polar plateau and the surrounding lowlands nearer the fringes of the Antarctic continent that causes the winds. As they race down from the higher polar elevation, the winds build in ferocity until they're nearly at gale strength by the time they rocket past those desperately flapping tents.

The six runners, three guides, and medical doctor ducked into one of these and were greeted by Doug, who would be the leader of our the expedition to the South Pole. Besides being a renowned mountain climber and extreme skier, Doug was also an avid runner.

"Welcome to summer camp," Doug said with a smile. Seeing us huddled and shivering, he quipped, "Think it's cold here? Just wait 'til we get to the Pole. It'll make this place feel like the Bahamas."

The man was built like a Viking. He had piercing blue eyes, a concrete chin, and bazookas for arms. Under his beanie was a mat of bushy blond hair framing his face like the mane of a lion. He looked like the kind of guy who wouldn't be rattled by a raging whiteout in the remotest place on earth.

We runners sat there freezing our butts off, wondering how we were possibly going to run 26.2 miles in these conditions. There were two other American runners, Don and Brent; two German runners, Raphael and Ute; and one from the Republic of Ireland, Richard.

Originally there was talk of up to thirty athletes participating in the event, but in the end it was just us six. Getting a small group to the South Pole is an expensive proposition, and the South Pole Marathon was likely a financial break-even proposition, at best. The expedition company handling logistics for the event, Adventure Network International (ANI), was the largest commercial enterprise bringing travelers to Antarctica. Besides us marathoners, they hosted climbers, meteorite hunters, and Pole taggers (people who simply flew to the South Pole to have their pictures taken next to it), some of whom were paying in excess of $35,000 to be there. Presumably the costs of the marathon could be absorbed by the many other groups ANI serviced. It's not uncommon for an organized running event (such as a 10K or a marathon) to lose money the first year and then recoup the losses in subsequent years. After all, this was the "inaugural" South Pole Marathon, which suggested it would be an ongoing event.

We runners all looked shaken by the savagery of the weather as Doug calmly addressed the group, reassuring us that the winds would soon ease and then we'd be off on another flight carrying us to the spot where our marathon would begin—26.2 miles from the South Pole.

A week later, we were still hunkered down at Patriot Hills. The weather hadn't let up one bit. No possibility of flights in or out.

We were going stir-crazy. Finding things to do in Patriot Hills was no mean feat. Just leaving the security of your tent was a trial. We spent a lot of time zipped up inside our goose-down mummy bags, urinating in pee-bottles. When we climbed out, we dressed in shivering stages, laboriously adding layers of protection against the bitter cold. They were not, to say the least, ideal running conditions. Far from it: running on Antarctica was perhaps the toughest physical challenge of my life.

No matter, I ran. It was bright daylight round the clock, so I sometimes went running at 2:00 A.M. as though it were high noon—there was little discernible difference. As challenging as it was to run in the soft snow, I kept it up all week, trying to harden myself for the upcoming event. I experimented with different layers of clothing and used specially designed waterproof running shoes to keep my feet dry. Using snowshoes would have made it easier, but I was hoping to complete the marathon without them. People had snowshoed to the South Pole before, but no one had ever run there.

The experimentation was essential. There was no precedent for running a marathon to the South Pole, and no one knew with certainty whether it could be done. I brought along every imaginable outdoor accessory, including a pair of top-of-the-line Tubbs racing snowshoes just in case it was impossible to run without relying on them. What I learned while training is that it wasn't impossible to run without snowshoes, just a lot tougher.

As the days mounted, Doug eventually organized a group training run in which everyone participated. It was only a 5-mile run, but it was difficult. We all ran in running shoes, and the snow was soft and yielding, making it demanding to keep a steady pace. It was a small taste of things to come. From this first experience of running any appreciable distance on the frigid, soft snow, I got the feeling that this "race" might ultimately be an exercise in survival more than anything else.

The next day, Brent, who was from Wyoming, began training using snowshoes. Richard borrowed a pair for the first time and realized the benefits. A controversy erupted. The snowshoes offered an advantage, and only Brent and I had them. We met as a group, and the consensus was that the use of snowshoes not be allowed during the marathon. This made sense. After all, only two of us had them. But more important, we wanted to be the first party ever to run a marathon to the South Pole. We hadn't come all this way to repeat history. I considered the matter settled, and packed away the snowshoes for good.

The days dragged on. A couple of the guys found a diversion in constructing a snow cave, and Richard spent the day adorning the interior with crude cave drawings of runners and wild animals. Two of our guides, Kris and Bean, started skiing and snowboarding the local peaks, and I soon found myself stealing away with the pair on snowmobiles, spending the afternoons carving up the nearby slopes.

My tolerance for the cold steadily improved. The snowboarding kept me active, and I continued to run. But even the frigid conditions at Patriot Hills wouldn't prepare me for the environment 600 miles away at the South Pole.

One day, the weather finally broke. We dashed into a modified Douglas DC-3 that quickly took off for the Pole before conditions could shut down again. We'd been delayed by more than a week at this point and were elated to be heading toward the start of the marathon. Only five runners were left, however. Raphael had decided that the risk of getting stuck even longer at the South Pole was too great, and he remained in Patriot Hills, awaiting the next flight home.

Flying around the Antarctic is treacherous. Modern avionics are of limited use in these parts; there's simply no aeronautical infrastructure, so pilots fly by old-fashioned Visual Flight Rules, or VFR. Basically, this means that if you can't see the ground, you can't land. And if you can't land, you've got to head back to where you came from . . . assuming you've got enough fuel to make it back. There's no shortage of mangled and burned-out aircraft wrecks on the continent.

As we were preparing to take off, I saw the co-pilot making the sign of the cross on his chest. It suddenly struck me how dangerous this whole endeavor was. Things could go terribly wrong in an instant, and the consequences could be grave. I never dwelled on danger; I focused on the task at hand. But it doesn't take a lot of introspection to admit that an element of risk, of serious physical harm, existed in almost all of the extreme adventures I undertook and was part of their appeal. Because of the elements and the remoteness, this South Pole marathon attempt was the most dangerous yet.

The plan was for the DC-3 to drop us off a marathon's distance from the Pole. As we landed on the spot, something seemed amiss. The plane fishtailed, erratically lurching and skipping. The pilot yanked up on the controls, and suddenly we were airborne again. We eventually landed on a flat expanse of crunchy snow 28.5 miles from the Pole. Nothing was ever mentioned about the incident, though I had a feeling that more had gone on than the flight crew let on to. At least we were safely on the ground.

It was eerie to think that possibly no human being had ever set foot where we were now standing. The polar plateau suspends reality; it's the most remote, most desolate, most inhospitable place on the planet. We had landed at 11,000 feet above sea level, but the effective elevation was closer to 13,000. The air is bone-dry, making Antarctica something like a huge desert—a frozen Sahara, where the temperature was –35 degrees Fahrenheit when we arrived. Nothing lives there, neither animal nor plant. Even the hardiest bacteria would have difficulty surviving. We were completely cut off from all other signs of life. It's as close to being on the moon as you can get while still on planet Earth.

We got busy erecting a small city around the plane. It would take us several days to acclimate to the elevation. At 4.5 percent body fat, I was certain I'd never adjust to the cold.

We got the tents set up. Then came the waiting. The hours crawl by when day and night look the same and when the landscape in every direction is flat and opaque white. A couple of us attempted a training run, but we scarcely covered a mile before turning back for fear of hypothermia and frostbite. Running on the frigid, crusty surface snow felt like tramping barefoot through a Freon marsh of styrofoam beads. Even with waterproof running shoes and neoprene socks, the cold cut right through to our feet. It would have been suicide to keep running in these conditions without greater protection. The experience scared the hell out of me.

Brent had written earlier, "I don't think folks really understand what it will be like trying to posthole twenty-six miles to the Pole." Damn straight. We could barely cover two miles, let alone a marathon. Our level of fitness would be supremely tested, no getting around that, but we needed to figure out a way to keep our feet from freezing if we were to have any chance of making it. I began experimenting by stuffing three Grabber Mycoal "shake-and-bake" heating pads—the kind used to keep ski boots warm—inside each shoe, two below the toes and one on top. It helped, a bit. They're advertised as staying warm for six hours, though in Antarctic conditions they gave out in half that time. Still, that was three hours that your toes didn't turn to icicles.

The sunny days and sunny nights bled together, the featureless landscape producing a sense of vertigo if you stared out at nothing for too long. I continued training, trying to maintain my fitness—and spirit—but the situation became more desperate and depressing with each passing day. We'd been stuck on the ice for three weeks now, hoping for a break in the weather that didn't seem like it would ever come. The stakes were getting progressively higher, each day away from family and work taking an increasing psychological toll.

And it wasn't just me who was feeling the strain—the group was increasingly fraying. The confinement of small tents, a single frozen bucket for a toilet, and nothing to do all day were wearing on everyone. Counting the flight crew, there were thirteen of us living in a tent the size of a small dormitory room. Gear and food were strewn everywhere. A small camping stove was kept going round the clock to melt drinking water, resulting in a damp condensation that dripped from the ceiling and created little frozen puddles on the floor. We needed to get on with this event soon. If only the weather would cooperate; but, unfortunately, Antarctica didn't have a history of cooperative weather.

The pressure on Doug to get things under way must have been tremendous. The cost of having a DC-3, flight crew, guides, and a physician all sitting idle was surely exorbitant. Adding to the strain, we had gotten the word that a group of Pole taggers were waiting in Patriot Hills for us to get the DC-3 back. These were folks that had paid a lot of money to be taken to the South Pole; they weren't the kind of people that were used to waiting in line, and we had the only plane that could get them there.

Doug remained focused and composed, but we could sense that if this marathon didn't happen soon, it wouldn't happen at all. With each passing hour, the costs mounted and the morale among the group slipped.

Our single contact with the outside world was an Iridium satellite phone. Reception was sporadic, but I managed to get through to my wife. I sat in the cabin of the DC-3, which was cold as a meat locker, and told her we were safe but were running a couple of *weeks* behind schedule. She was characteristically supportive as we spoke, and I could hear Alexandria and Nicholas in the background asking, "Is it Daddy? Is it Daddy?"

"How is everyone?" I asked through the static.

"We're doing fine," she assured me. "But the kids miss you. I miss you, too. Is everything all right?"

"I think so. Doug and the guides are competent, but there's a lot that's beyond our contol. And running a marathon in these conditions is going to be scary, if it's even possible at all. No one's gone more than a mile away from camp yet."

"Please be safe," she said.

I just bit my lip. There was no way I could offer any assurances on that one.

I asked if she wouldn't mind contacting my office. "I'm sure they'll be happy to hear an update," she said.

Thankfully, I had an understanding boss. I'd just about burned through all my accrued vacation days, and it wasn't looking like I'd be home anytime soon.

I told Julie that I loved her, and she wished us all well. "Be careful," she said.

"I'll do my best. Hug those kids for me, and I'll see you all soon."

The guilt and loneliness of being away from my family and job gnawed at me like never before. The stakes were getting higher with each passing day. There were responsibilities—as a father and co-worker—that I needed to uphold, and I was stuck in Antarctica, trying to run a marathon. I longed to get this event under way and return home. In one piece.

The dreariness of the situation weighed heavily on me. Though stressing about it wasn't going to change anything, we weren't going anywhere. So I called my training buddy, Christopher Gaylord, for a little levity. We laughed hysterically at the grimness of my predicament. I told him about the exploded beer cans lying on the floor of the plane, with the frozen froth clinging to the walls like spray-on insulation; about trying to brush our teeth with frozen toothpaste that wouldn't thaw unless you slept with the tube in your mummy bag; and about our delightful meals, "cooked" on a small camping stove that could barely get the water warm enough to heat our dehydrated rice, meat, and vegetables. They were soggy on the outside and crunchy in the middle. The particles that weren't cooked fermented pleasantly in our stomachs.

"The air inside our tent doesn't smell like roses," I said.

"Maybe you can float the tent home," Gaylord said, "like a big helium balloon."

It sure would beat running at this point.

After more days of waiting, the weather finally yielded enough for Doug to decide it was time to attempt the marathon. Small yellow mile-markers had been set up along the way by a party that had left from the Pole on snowmobiles and worked their way out to us. We were supposed to follow these markers (when we could see them). The gun went off, and the race was on.

We didn't get very far. Not two hours into it, the visibility shut down and conditions deteriorated. The race was quickly called off. It was another harsh disappointment and a sobering learning experience. Two of the runners, Don and Ute, had covered fewer than 3 miles in that time. At that pace, it'd take them over seventeen hours to finish the marathon. They'd likely succumb to exposure first.

After the first race attempt, in an e-mail sent via satellite from our tent, Don described the situation like this:

> By the time we got to the 2-mile mark, we had a hard time seeing the marker wands in front of us. We got almost to the 3-mile mark where Doug was waiting for us, visibility was falling, and the world was white from ground to sky. As Doug turned around on the snowmobile to tell us that the race was cancelled, he lost his equilibrium and fell off. That's what happens when your whole world is the same color and you're in motion. He picked us up and we headed back toward the start. We ended up driving in circles trying to find the way back to the DC-3.

The experience left him apprehensive. "This is going to be brutal," he wrote, and concluded soberly, "Finishing a marathon in these conditions could be more dangerous than I bargained for."

Something had to change. That demoralizing first attempt convinced the group that our whole concept of the marathon had to be radically rethought. The ferocity of the conditions demanded it. Don and Ute decided to run a half-marathon instead.

That left only three of us running the marathon. Then Brent announced that he would be using his snowshoes. "I know my limitations," he said. He was an experienced runner and snowshoer, so I was inclined to trust his judgment.

Then Richard approached me in our tent and asked if he could borrow my snowshoes. Did this mean that what we had decided upon in Patriot Hills was out the window? That the race was off and all we were trying to do at this point was complete the endeavor in any way we could? Safety had become the primary concern.

"Sure, man," I said, digging out the snowshoes from the bottom of my bag and handing them to him, "whatever it takes."

After the conclusion of the event, in a message to a buddy, Brent put it this way: "Once we arrived at the polar plateau, it was decided the run would not be a race, but an expedition run in which all team members agreed to stay together for safety reasons. Everybody made sacrifices in order to make it happen. It was a total team effort."

Even though he wouldn't be running the full marathon, Don remained upbeat. "Ute and I would fly to the Pole and do a half-marathon that could be easily monitored," he wrote in another satellite e-mail from our tent. "Brent and Richard would wear snowshoes, Dean would wear just running shoes. The three of them would have to stay close together, expedition style." He must have been disappointed that he wasn't doing the entire marathon, but he showed valor in choosing to concede on the side of safety.

Doug and one of our guides, Kris, would be supporting our marathon efforts on snowmobile. Given the savagery of the conditions, we were instructed to stay within eyesight of one another so that we could be safely monitored. The plan was for me to run my ass off and, I hoped, stay up with the guys wearing snowshoes. It didn't sound entirely like a "team" effort to me, but I was willing to give it my best shot. This was probably our last chance; if we failed here, we would likely be forced to abandon the effort and return home without finishing anything.

I knew I'd have to push very hard from the onset, so as not to slow the group down. My calculations were that I could complete the course in five to six hours wearing snowshoes. Without them, I wasn't sure how long it would take, or if I could even make it.

The group left the tent like men on a mission. But we only made it to the edge of camp. The snowmobiles wouldn't start. The carburetors apparently hadn't been adjusted to the higher elevation of the polar plateau and the engines wouldn't turn over, or were frozen, or had voodoo spirits infesting them, or whatever . . . the damn things just wouldn't start. It was another delay as the flight mechanic began inspecting the internal workings.

Eventually he was able to jury-rig the starter, and he got the engines turned over. How long they would run for, and if they would restart if they stalled midway through the marathon, was anybody's guess. We wanted to get this thing going and were getting reckless. I could sense Doug's unease. This was a man who had high standards where safety was concerned.

What transpired during our second attempt at a marathon is largely a frigid blur. Luckily, much of it was captured on videotape. As Brent and Richard were busily adjusting their snowshoes and getting them strapped on, I stood bouncing and shivering in the freezing temperatures trying to stay warm. "I'm freezing," I said to the group. "I'm going to start moving." I knew with their snowshoes they'd have no problem catching up.

"Me, too," Richard said, having affixed the snowshoes and joining in with me. "God help us all." Those are the last words that were said before we began trudging forward into the pallid abyss, heads down to deflect the incomprehensible cold.

Since this was the second, and likely last, attempt at the marathon, Doug was hyper-astute in making sure everything was going well at an early stage. Scarcely a mile into it, he was already inquiring about our progress, asking Richard if the snowshoes were helping. "Yeah," Richard said to the camera, "it makes a difference, all right."

That was good. Our initial prospects of completing the event this time around looked more encouraging than they had the first time. Now it would just be up to me to keep up with the group in my running shoes, which was no small chore.

I'd started out briskly in hopes of regenerating some of the internal body heat that was lost while standing idle at the start. Running hard helped to warm my core body temperature, but no amount of effort could keep my feet warm. Without the platform of a snowshoe to land on, I kept dunking my foot directly into the frigid ice pack below the surface where the temperature was a uniform –54 degrees, and I was forced to stop along the way to change the heating pads in my running shoes. Replacing the three pads in each shoe was costing time, and I'd quickly lose body heat when I stopped, but it was a necessary evil. Without fresh heating pads, frostbite was inevitable.

We slogged along within eyesight of one another for much of the first half of the marathon. I was pushing as hard as I could to keep up, and it was draining. I would run ahead and stop to change heating pads, and the others would catch up—like a quasi-hare-and-tortoise routine—and then I'd charge out again, trying to recapture some of the body heat that was lost from the pit stop. A couple of times I asked Doug if the group was sticking close enough to be safely monitored. He reassured me that things were fine. That was comforting, because I was incapable of going much faster.

As the run progressed, my goggles would instantaneously fog whenever I stopped. The cumulative moisture buildup resulted in instant condensation. If I removed my goggles so that I could see, my eyes would start to water profusely and the tears would painfully freeze. So I left the goggles on and fumbled in the haze.

We runners exchanged few words along the way— primarily just grumbles about the cold (it was approaching –40 degrees). Talking was difficult with a "gorilla mask" covering your mouth and nose. You had to wear one, though. Breathing the superchilled air directly could freeze your trachea.

By mile 17, icicles had formed under my neoprene face mask, limiting my ability to eat or drink—or even move my head. My progress in the soft snow was brutally slow as my feet sank deeper into the yielding surface the harder I pushed off. It felt like I was running at full capacity, every muscle in my body working overtime, but with the snow sucking me down I was barely inching forward. By mile 18, I began having serious doubts about whether I could complete the marathon. My heart raced, but I scarcely covered any ground.

I kept going, numbly.

At the 20-mile mark, my fingers were so cold that I couldn't clench my fists. I was unable to change the heating pads in my shoes at this point; I didn't have the dexterity left. The body heat I was generating by running as hard as I could didn't account for much in the sub-zero temperatures. The cold was winning. It seeped in through every seam of my clothing.

When it's cold beyond comprehension, you start losing your natural instincts. *Am I freezing? No, things are fine. Wait a minute, I can't feel my toes! Should I stop?* When the temperatures are so low, just a few minutes of poor judgment can cost body parts. Unlike the heat of Death Valley, where you can seek reprieve in the shade, there was no escape from the polar cold, no place to hide.

The altitude was another factor, and one we'd underestimated in our planning. Thinking only of the relative flatness of the polar plateau, we'd failed to prepare for running at the elevation of a significant mountain. I was sucking the frigid, oxygen-poor air at 11,000 feet above sea level through a neoprene muffler that had frozen solid. Every breath was like trying to suck an ice cube through a straw. I was running in the most desolate, open expanse on the planet, suffocating.

What kept me going? Easy. It is what I lived for. The adventure. The challenge of pushing the human body beyond reality. Not only had a marathon to the South Pole never been run before, but plenty of people doubted it could be done, said it would be impossible. I was out to prove that it could be done, regardless of how irrational, how improbable, how dangerous the effort was. That it was obliterating me in the process only heightened my fighting spirit. I had something to prove, if only to myself: that it *could* be done, that nothing was impossible.

At mile 22, my face mask had become a solid block of ice. My breath had dampened it, and it froze stiff. Eating and drinking became impossible; nothing could reach my mouth through the frozen block. But just as worrisome as the inability to eat or drink was the small gap that had developed between my goggles and face mask. The arctic air sneaked through unabated, searing the tissue along my upper left cheek. With the face mask now completely frozen and immovable, it was impossible to seal off the crack. It felt like Novocain was being injected into my cheek. First came the sting of the needle being inserted, then the area tingled and went numb.

This is how people die in the cold. They push too hard and don't realize it until they've gone past the point of no return. The situation had gotten critical. Every step forward came at a mounting price. My muscles were slowly running out of fuel, and there was no way of getting food into my mouth. The vicious air was attacking my face, so I ran with my head hunched over as far as possible in an effort to deflect the biting headwind and prevent further tissue damage. I slogged forward, trying to keep my feet moving through the sinking surface, ignoring the stinging and hoping that I could reach the Pole before having to curl into a ball on the snow.

Periodically, I glanced up in hopes of seeing something. Not only was the horizon difficult to gauge, but my goggles were fogged and frozen, creating a restrictive tunnel vision. I could see nothing but white in every direction.

There was no way to look at my wristwatch without removing a mitten, which was out of the question at this point. Even if I could get to my watch, deciphering the time through these clouded goggles might very well be impossible. We had been out here a long time, that much was certain. Even while I ran at full capacity, the soft snow, which sometimes swallowed an entire foot, bogged me down so badly that it was grueling maintaining a fifteen-minute-mile pace—about the speed of a brisk walk on a hard surface. I ran as hard as I could, but barely moved forward. Given the stops to change the heating pads in my shoes, I guessed that we'd been going at it for close to eight hours. Usually I could run two marathons in that time, even on the most demanding course. But not here.

My mind was focused on one thing this entire time: getting through the ordeal in one piece. There were no flashbacks or daydreams, no existential thoughts: the intensity of the conditions and the unrelenting physical demands placed upon me commanded all of my attention. And the situation was rapidly becoming perilous.

Doug and Kris were nowhere to be seen. Had their snowmobiles stalled? Were they lost? It was difficult to decipher anything. The snowmobiles would be next to me at points along the way, and then I wouldn't see them for long stretches of time. *If I were to crumple in a heap on the snow, would they ever find me?* One of our guides, Bean, was an experienced back-country pioneer and had instructed us to always save 10 percent of our energy in case something unforeseen occurred. I had long since tapped into that reserve. In fact, I was running on empty by now.

I kept scanning the horizon, hoping to spot something, anything. Still only white. Then, remarkably, something emerged in the distance. One glance up, there was nothing; the next, there appeared to be something dark on the horizon. Yes, something was out there all right. Elated, I began to sprint. I couldn't imagine it being anything but the Pole; what else could be out here? The quicker I got there, the less frostbite damage my face would sustain and the sooner I could get new heating pads in my shoes and food in my mouth. It was a reckless all-or-nothing burst; if this little spot in the distance wasn't the finish, I was in trouble.

Thank God, it was. The marker at the South Pole is, well, a pole. A red-and-white-striped pole, like outside an old-fashioned barbershop. It was well past midnight as I charged toward it, heaving my chest forward in an attempt to propel my weary legs over the last bit of course. My goggles were entirely frozen over, and it was difficult to decipher anything. A snowmobile, or something, appeared before me. Actually it was Don, running in the opposite direction for some reason. At the last second I saw his hand in the air, and we high-fived each other. Apparently he was still running the half-marathon. I was in no condition to stop and ask, and we ran right past each other and kept going our own ways.

The midnight sun shone brightly overhead, bedazzling the snow as I crossed under the makeshift finish line, throwing my exhausted arms up in celebration. It had taken nine hours and eighteen minutes to reach, and it had nearly killed me. My muscles trembled and my face felt like someone was holding a match to it—I couldn't tell whether it was hot or cold. I needed to get to shelter and get something warm in my system.

They put me on a snowmobile and shuttled me to a nearby tent, where a camp stove was heating water. Brent came in a minute later. He was thrashing and twisting—apparently his face mask was stuck to his head—and he knocked over the stove, spilling fuel across the tent floor. The floor ignited, and a fire quickly erupted inside the tent.

Crossing the finish line

One of the guides saw what had happened and rushed over to put out the flames. After extinguishing the fire, he tended to Brent. The face mask was frozen in place, so it had to be cut off his head with a pair of scissors.

All the while, I was dealing with the frostbite on my cheeks and nose, applying ointment and trying to warm the area. My shoes were off, and I'd wrapped my feet in a goose-down sleeping bag, trying to bring back some of the circulation.

Richard's hip flexors had seized up completely, and he had succumbed to hypothermia. He was partially snow-blind and was suffering from frostbite; he eventually received medical attention for both of those conditions and for exhaustion. The doctor administered four liters of IV fluid into Richard's arm to help revive him.

It seemed like a pretty heavy toll to pay, but, considering what we had just done, things could have been much worse. Any goal worth achieving involves an element of risk. Running a marathon to the bottom of the earth was clearly an extreme case, but the higher the risk, the grander the sense of satisfaction from accomplishing what you set out to do. We did it. And lived.

The next morning, before we left the Pole, Don had a wild idea: "Let's run around the world naked." What he meant is that if we ran around the barber pole, we'd actually be circumventing the globe—at its smallest circumference, of course.

Despite my frostbite, I wasn't about to miss this one. So the two of us stripped to our boots and did a (quick) loop around the Pole. Now I have the dubious distinction of being the first and only person ever to run a marathon to the South Pole in running shoes, and one of only two to run around the world naked. Luckily I'd emerged from both with all appendages intact.

Just after a run around the world

ANI declared all participants equal winners and recognized each for having completed a unique challenge,
and the world's inaugural South Pole Marathon was,
with all its obstacles and compromises, one for the history books. Lord knows if there'd be a second one any
time soon, if ever. Maybe it was just as well. It had taken
nearly a month of being stuck on the ice and two tries to
complete the event. We were at the top of our game,
and we still barely pulled it off. The next group might
not be so fortunate.

Waiting at the airport in Chile were a handful of local
press. They wanted to know if I was the guy who had
run to the South Pole in his tennis shoes, as they put it.
One of the reporters interviewing me asked how I knew
I could make it. I explained to him that I didn't know if

I could make it, and that is what made the adventure so grand. *"Fantástico!"* He laughed.

The flight home was overbooked and crowded. Our plane broke down in Lima, and we sat in the sweltering midsummer heat for five hours. It was a shock to my system, having just left the Antarctic sub-zero temperatures and now sitting in the tropics.

Four flights and thirty-nine hours later, I arrived home, elated that I'd made it in time. It was Alexandria's seventh birthday.

Her party was in full swing as I tiptoed through the door, the house filled with balloons, giggling girls, and birthday cake. "Surprise!" I said.

"Daddy!" she screamed, and came running over to me. We hugged and she laughed in delight; I, on the other hand, wept like a child. The emotion of seeing my family after being stranded at the bottom of the earth simply overcame me.

The kids at the party wanted to know what those funny marks on my face were all about. I explained that it was called frostbite—"kind of like sunburn, only for the opposite reason," I told them.

That night I read *Charlotte's Web* to Alexandria and Nicholas. They fell asleep before I finished the second page, just like old times. I carried them to their beds, tucked them in, and quietly kissed them good night. Julie and I shared a toast and ordered Thai food from our favorite restaurant.

"You look good," she said, "vibrant."

"You're not looking too bad yourself," I said with a wink.

"Are you flirting with me?"

"No, I'm making a full-on pass at you. I've been living in a refrigerated tent for the past month in the middle of nowhere."

"Come here, Iceman," she joked.

And for the first time since leaving home, I began to thaw out.

The next morning I awoke before dawn, doing my best not to wake Julie, and went for a run out to the Golden Gate Bridge before work. The sun was coming up, the fishing boats were heading out to sea, the birds were chirping. It'd been a month since I'd heard a bird sing, and I realized that going close to the edge gives you a newfound appreciation of the familiar. Nothing gets taken for granted, and you see the world through fresh eyes. Running beyond the limits was my form of renewal.

Would I ever return to Antarctica? I've returned plenty of times in my mind. It's not the kind of experience you soon forget. Would I ever physically return? In a heartbeat. I've stayed in close contact with Doug, and he's always planning the next grand adventure.

I'd run across Death Valley in the middle of summer, and now I'd run to the coldest place on earth; it might be tough bettering that. But I kept searching for something even more intense.

It's just the way an ultramarathoner's mind works.

Chapter 13

The Ultra-Endurance World

Recovery is overrated.

—Jim Vernon

1993–2004

Just as the boundaries of technology are being pushed at an accelerated rate, so, too, are the frontiers of human endurance. The big difference is that the gains in human physical achievement are going largely unnoticed.

Even while participation in 10Ks and marathons is on the rise, 100-mile footraces remain almost unknown to the general public. The level of corporate sponsorship and media coverage of just one major U.S. marathon, like Boston or Chicago, would dwarf that of all ultra-endurance events combined. And when comparing any running event to a popular spectator sport, like football or baseball, the level of endorsements isn't even a blip on the radar.

And I like that.

Runners are real people. They don't run for money or recognition, they do it out of passion. Most have day jobs that pay the bills, and running is a labor of love. Ultrarunners take it to the next level. Training to run 100 miles while working nine-to-five requires a phenomenal level of commitment and determination. It's a select breed that can withstand the tremendous physical and emotional toll that performing on such a level demands. Without discipline to rise before dawn and pound out the miles, you'll never make it. If the fire in your heart isn't strong, there's no point trying.

Most ultra-endurance races are staged on a shoestring budget by people who do it because they love the sport. Unlike a sanctioned marathon, with frequent water-stops along the way, most ultramarathons have limited access to supplies. I remember one gritty 50-miler I participated in where the only support on the course was a water hose at the halfway point. A new ultrarunner griped about having to wait in line to get water. "If you don't want to wait in line," the race director suggested, "get there first."

Over the years, I've developed numerous friendships in the ultra-endurance underground. Many of these athletes are reserved and keep largely to themselves. Running for twenty-four hours at a time doesn't lend itself to a robust social schedule. Some are running from the bottle. Some are running from past transgressions. Most are just hyper-energetic adrenaline junkies out to savor life to the last drop; life's super-users, if you will. Whatever the case may be, all have an internal fire that burns strong, for one reason or another.

John Medinger, the president of the Western States Endurance Run Foundation, hosts the annual 101st Mile Party to honor those "astounding studs and studettes" who have successfully completed a 100-mile endurance run in the past season. The celebration kicks off with a "casual" 9-mile trail run. Over the years, I've noticed an emerging trend at this gathering: Many of the honorees have completed not just one 100-mile endurance race during the year, they've completed two or more. This past season, for instance, I completed six events of 100 miles or longer, making it effectively a 788th Mile Party for this kid. That's like racing from Washington, D.C., to Florida. If you follow the traditional running adage that you need one week of recovery for every mile you race, I should be spending the next fourteen and one-half years resting from this past summer alone.

Guess it's time to start drinking.

Like most others at the party, I was a recreational drinker with a running problem. As I entered Medinger's house and searched for beer, the energy emitted by the crowd was bouncing off the walls like electrons. The place was buzzing with endorphins. Yet a certain humility also pervades the group, as though these people don't need to express their prowess publicly. Their achievements speak for themselves.

"Hey, Med," I address the host, "seen Rocket?"

"No, Karno."

That's how we seem to converse—in compact sound bites, as if using whole names and complete sentences requires too much energy expenditure. Better to conserve it for use elsewhere.

"Check food table," he concludes. "Probably there."

I never do locate the man, because once I find food and drink I scarcely move an inch—except to stuff another nugget in my mouth. It feels bizarre elbowing people and fighting for position around the food table. The competition is fierce. As soon as something new arrives, all conversation ceases and every last crumb is ferociously devoured. We stand about gorging ourselves like grizzlies, yet no one in the room has body fat in excess of single digits. Where does it all go?

On the trail, no doubt, chasing some unprecedented feat of endurance.

The 101st Mile Party is for the hard-core group, but over the years I've also inducted a handful of new recruits into the ranks of ultra-endurance running. Sadly, most are now excommunicated and have never forgiven me for dragging them into the sport. One ex-friend ran 60 miles with me all night. He hasn't run a day since. That was four years ago.

But those select few that have persisted have developed into remarkable endurance athletes. Topher Gaylord first ran with me for a brief stretch during my attempt to run 199 miles nonstop. He got hooked and signed up for a 50-kilometer race shortly after that. When he asked me how to run an ultramarathon (defined as any distance beyond a marathon, which is 26.2 miles), I instructed him to puff out his chest, put one foot in front of the other, and don't stop till he'd crossed the finish line.

"That's it?" he asked.

"Yep," I said, "nothing to it."

Running his first ultramarathon temporarily crippled him. The pounding left him unable to walk up stairs. Still, he completed the event, which showed promise. Most people in his condition would have bailed long before reaching the finish line. His progress during the latter part of the run was so slow that nearly the entire field passed him, and he finished near the back of the pack.

Sitting at his plush office desk the week after, he received an envelope in the mail from me. His boss had walked in and Topher was telling him about the rigors of running 50 kilometers as he opened his mail. Inside my envelope was a brief note and a small cylindrical tube. Toph read the note aloud:

Gaylord,

After your effort last weekend, I thought you might be needing this.
Your friend,
Karno

Thinking it was a victory cigar, he pulled it out to show his boss.

It was a tampon.

He's worked hard to live down that moment. Now that he's completed the Western States Endurance Run a fourth time, I think he has.

Even among the fittest of the fit, ultra-endurance athletes remain a freakish anomaly. People can understand running a marathon, but running four or five back to back, running for forty-eight hours straight, or running in the hottest and coldest places on earth transcends rational thought. It contradicts people's sense of what is possible.

"Why haven't I ever heard of this before?" is a common response. "It's remarkable."

The mainstream press doesn't focus much on ultra-endurance sports, probably because they're relatively new and the media are doing just fine covering baseball, basketball, and football, thank you. But this is changing. Slowly.

How *Sports Illustrated Women* found my name remains somewhat of a mystery. Of all the athletes profiled in their "Sexiest Men in Sports" issue, I was the only runner. One would think they'd choose some mainstream track star—a sprinter or hurdler—not some obscure

Photo courtesy of Bob Scott

Sports Illustrated Women's
"Sexiest Men in Sports" issue

extreme-endurance dude most Americans have never heard of whose sport is beyond comprehension.

My running friends certainly gave me plenty of grief for appearing in the *Sports Illustrated Women*'s "swimsuit issue," as they called it. And the one time that *Runner's World* magazine decided to mention my participation in the Western States Endurance Run, it wrote that the big question is: "What will he be wearing?"

Maybe being an underground athlete isn't such a bad thing after all.

The fallout from the "Sexiest Men in Sports" appointment, however, was entirely confined to my training pals poking fun at me. There are no "endurance groupies," as far as I can tell. The women in the sport are just as tough as the men. Sometimes tougher. They're more interested in getting to the finish line before me than getting my phone number. The few times I have been hit on, it's been for a PowerBar or some extra water. And if I didn't produce the desired request quickly, they were gone. No time for a man to slow them down.

When it gets right down to it, the levels of commitment and devotion required to excel as an ultra-endurance athlete are all-consuming. Beyond running 80 to 120 miles per week, along with mountain biking, surfing, and windsurfing regularly, my routine consists of 200 push-ups, 50 pull-ups, and 400 sit-ups—twice a day. Sure, I'm ripped, but not for the sake of vanity. A chiseled build comes as a by-product of my passions. I couldn't see the utility of having such brawn if not to put it to good use pushing the body to inconceivable extremes.

Excessive as my routine may sound, there are others who are just as fanatical. I know of runners who've trained for Badwater by doing a thousand sit-ups daily, *inside a sauna!* That may sound overzealous, but when you're standing at the start of some daunting ultra-endurance slugfest, it's psychologically comforting to know that you haven't skimped on your preparation. Anything less than total commitment won't cut it.

It's also important to train your body to run all night,

and still go strong the next day. Once I ran from our house in San Francisco to the start of the Napa Valley Marathon (100 miles in eighteen hours, straight through the night), arrived five minutes before the start, and then ran the marathon (in 3:15). These are the sorts of things we do as ultrarunners.

Fathering two kids hasn't slowed me down. Quite the contrary, it's kept me on my toes. Now I really have something to prove: that it's possible to be a loving, caring, and responsible father and a competitive athlete at the same time; that nice guys can finish first.

Sure, there have been sacrifices along the way. Regrettably, I've lost touch with many old friends and acquaintances, never having time to connect any longer. And often I find myself living on four hours of sleep a night for weeks on end, trying to keep the dynamics of family, work, and running in balance. Forgoing sleep is the only way I've figured out how to fit it all in. I'm not willing to compromise my family time, but I'm not willing to let my level of fitness slip, either. Yes, I confess, there is a certain level of selfishness involved. A lot of what I do is for my own personal fulfillment. Still, I think I'm a better man for it. Over the years, I've only missed one of my son's basketball games on account of my running, and I've made every soccer game—even if sometimes I've run there.

Truth is, I view running as the savior that's brought my family together. Not only has running provided my restless energy with an outlet, it has given us a common goal to rally around. The kids love traveling to events and helping with the preparation and crewing. They've joined in my victories and shared in the disappointment of defeat. They've witness firsthand the struggles and sacrifices required to achieve success. "Dreams can come true," I've told them, "especially if you train hard enough."

And my parents are fully engaged. They rarely miss a big event. We've grown closer as a family as a result, and we've grown as individuals as well. Running great distances has proven to be a powerful tonic for the soul . . . and not just mine. We've created new memories that have helped to ease the pain of past sadness. Nothing can replace the loss of my sister, but she would be proud of how we've united as a family, rekindled the fire and kept it burning . . . and burning strong.

My brother Kraig still thinks my extreme running is at the fringe of rationality. But at least now we can laugh about it, and we do often.

So I had no intentions of letting up. After completing the Badwater Ultramarathon, I still longed to test the limits of my endurance. "What's next?" I continued to question. There had to be another challenge to sink my teeth into beyond Badwater. Something grander, more obscure, more daunting. But what? What could possibly be tougher than the world's toughest footrace? I wanted to do something more demanding than anything I'd done before.

Why? Because I was just getting warmed up.

Chapter 14

The Relay

Start slow, then taper off.

— Walt Stack,
Bay Area running legend

Marin County, California
Saturday morning, September 30, 2000

Seven hours had transpired since I'd departed the Mother Ship back in Napa. My family was asleep, camping for the night, as I continued running onward. It had taken some searching, and creativity, to find something beyond Badwater, but eventually I'd uncovered the ultimate challenge.

As the name would imply, The Relay is just that: a relay race. In my quest for the next adventure, I'd overlooked that central point. This 199-mile footrace starts in Calistoga and ends at the beach in Santa Cruz, the course being divided into thirty-six discrete legs of about 5.5 miles apiece. All members of each twelve-person team are responsible for running three of these legs at various points along the way, their crew van transporting the others up the road to the next exchange, where the baton will be passed along to a different runner.

For them, in other words, it was a relay race.

I'd opted to run a slightly different race, attempting to tackle the entire 199 miles by myself. A team of one.

When I first contacted the founder of The Relay, Jeff Shapiro, M.D., he probably thought I was nuts when I explained that since I couldn't find eleven friends to run with, I'd do the race solo. When I persisted, even as he offered to try and help locate eleven other runners, he clearly thought it was a prank call. "Suuure," he said.

I took his response as legitimate, sent in my entry form, and here I was, running The Relay, solo. I was even leading the pack, figuratively. Race starts were staggered based on the projected speed of your team, so that all teams would finish roughly at the same time. Since I was certainly the slowest "team" of all, my start time was set the day before the others. I had left Calistoga at 5:00 P.M. on Friday after work; the teams didn't start until Saturday morning.

In my pocket was the picture of a little girl, Elizabeth Wood. I pulled out the picture and looked at it again. The edges were getting tattered, but the image still stirred me. It was obviously taken at the hospital, but she looked filled with life, despite being in critical condition. She did not look ready to leave this world, and I was committed to doing whatever I could to help keep her here. I tucked the picture back in my pocket for safe-keeping and continued running along.

After having the existential pizza-delivery dude (he'd asked me *"Why?"* I do what I do) deliver that roadside supreme pizza, cheesecake, and coffee, my spirits and energy level soared, and I ran along at a decent clip. Having passed through the town of Petaluma, the road meandered west into the rural ranchlands of Marin County, and I kept running, well off the beaten path.

The Relay course didn't follow the most direct route to Santa Cruz but opted instead for a safer back-country alternative to the heavily trafficked main thoroughfares. Besides being safer, it was also more picturesque. The light of the full moon covered the hills in a silvery varnish. It was 3:00 A.M., and although I was equipped with an LED headlamp and a halogen hand-held flashlight, that brilliant moon rendered them unnecessary.

Dr. Shapiro planned The Relay for a full moon; it was safer. Come sunrise, some two hundred teams of twelve runners would start in Calistoga and follow me along this 199-mile route to Santa Cruz. They would run all night and reach the beach in Santa Cruz on Sunday afternoon. I would run all night two nights in a row and reach the beach in Santa Cruz around the same time . . . if everything went as planned, which was pretty wishful thinking.

The buzzing of my cell phone cracked the silence.

"Karno!" my friend Scotty screamed. Other voices yelled in the background. "Karno, where are you?"

"I'm just past Petaluma. Where are you?"

"Doing the city, buddy, as you should be on Friday night." I heard a voice call out, "'Nother round!"

"You still going to meet me in the morning?" I asked.

"Yep," Scotty answered. "Got to get in my exercise."

"Don't forget, it's a buck a mile."

"Yeah, yeah. Just keep that cell phone on, I'll track you down."

Behind him voices cheered, "Go, Karno! Run!"

A call like that could carry me five or six miles before the struggling to keep running resumed. I'd been running now for ten hours straight since departing Calistoga, and the going was getting tougher. People think I'm crazy to put myself through such torture, though I would argue otherwise. Somewhere along the line we seem to have confused comfort with happiness. I've now come to believe that quite the opposite is the case. Dostoyevsky had it right: "Suffering is the sole origin of consciousness." Never are my senses more engaged than when the pain sets in. There is magic in misery. Just ask any runner.

Time passed and I kept running. Two hours elapsed, and there was scarcely another sign of civilization. Sometimes I'd hear a cow moo. Occasionally I'd be surprised by the skittish eyes of a deer or raccoon crossing the road. Otherwise the world, at three in the morning, was still.

Running straight through the night, I'd watched the

bluish moon rise, grow big and bright and white in the sky, crest midnight, and then begin its yellowy descent to the distant horizon. All the while, I ran, stopping only to retie my shoelace.

Dawn emerged strikingly clear, not a cloud in the morning sky. I carried a lightweight jacket with me, but there was no need for it. I'd run through the night in a short-sleeved shirt, which was all I needed to stay warm—almost too warm. As the sun rose, the air around me quickly began heating. It was going to be a very warm weekend, with temperatures likely reaching the 90s. Bummer.

Heat is the runner's enemy. Running generates tremendous internal heat and forces the body to work doubly hard to keep the muscles cool. When outside temperatures rise, the stress on the body is multiplied.

For me, heat is particularly menacing. Living in San Francisco limits one's exposure to warmth—hypothermia is a more likely concern. Complicating matters, I'm bulky. Muscles produce heat, and since I'm into a variety of outdoor sports, my upper body is pretty well developed. Carrying that extra bulk is not a good quality for a runner; a wiry body produces less heat. Yet some things in life are worth the sacrifice. I wasn't about to stop doing the others sports I loved just to drop some upper-body mass.

I combed my fingers through my short, dark hair, which was a different sort of sacrifice. Given my druthers, I'd wear it longer—I'd let the stubble on my face flourish for a few extra days before shaving, too—but my lifestyle had already deviated sufficiently from convention. I couldn't control my impulse to migrate like a wildebeest periodically, but I could keep my hair neatly trimmed and my face cleanly shaven. Probably best to maintain at least the overt signs of corporate conformity. After all, I did have a wife and family to support.

The first round of teams had left Calistoga by now. Every half-hour throughout the day, a new round of teams would leave the starting gate and begin the trek south. It was difficult to conceive that these same desolate back-country roads I had just traversed would soon be crowded with hundreds of runners and crew vehicles, all 199 miles to Santa Cruz. The Relay bills itself as "California's Longest Party." If your idea of fun is running all weekend and sharing a crew vehicle with eleven stinky teammates, it probably doesn't get any better.

I was running through the Nicasio Valley, leg 14 of the course, when my cell phone rang again.

"Hello, son," my dad said. "How are you?"

"Just fine. It's a magnificent morning. How did you guys sleep last night?" I asked.

"Really well," he said. "We found this great little campsite up in the hills above Napa."

Pulling an all-nighter had become routine for me. The first time I'd attempted to run all night, it was a battle to stay awake and coherent. Subsequent outings proved progressively less traumatizing. Now I was conditioned to the point where running straight through the night was standard operating procedure, and an experience I quite enjoyed, actually.

"How are the kids?"

"They're cooking breakfast, having a ball. Where you at?"

"I'm heading for San Geronimo. Want to meet in Sausalito for lunch?"

"Sounds good," he said. "We'll call you soon."

San Geronimo is some 20 miles beyond Petaluma. The sun crested the horizon as I made my way into town. One of the beautiful things about approaching San Geronimo from the west is that the first commercial enclave you come to has a 7-Eleven. It was time to refuel.

With a grande microwavable burrito, a bag of Doritos, two cinnamon buns, a massive cherry Slurpee, and four packets of salt in hand, I exited with a wide smile. Sitting on the curb in front of the store was the first time in fifteen hours I'd been off my feet.

The first order of business was sugar. My normal training diet was a strict regime of slow-carbohydrate foods, high-quality protein, and good fats. Since becoming a devoted endurance athlete, I'd followed what could best be described as a controlled-carb diet, consuming only carbohydrates that were metabolized slowly and provided lasting energy. All simple sugars had been completely eliminated; a single jelly bean could send me into a glycemic tizzy.

But on these extended outings, my body craved sugar. My system was like a steam locomotive: the more fuel that was dumped into the boiler room, the greater the output. I found it difficult to consume enough calories by eating healthy foods alone. My calculations were that I burned 600 calories an hour. If I were to run for forty-eight hours, I needed to consume a whopping 28,800 calories to match my expenditure. Healthy foods are typically less calorie-dense, because the natural fiber is left in place and not stripped away. Given this additional bulk, it would be impossible to stuff 28,800 calories of healthy food into my gut. The sheer mass would bloat a hippopotamus! So I resort to eating highly refined, richly sweetened, calorie-dense foods. Pastries, doughnuts, candy; the more calorie-packed, the better. (A food log is posted in the Appendix on page 280. This diet is not to be emulated; it's a rare indulgence for a fanatical extreme endurance athlete.)

You also deplete your system of sodium when running long distances, especially when it's warm. So, along with the sugar for energy, it's crucial to replace the lost sodium. I dumped four packets of salt into the Slurpee and stirred it all up. A sweet 'n' salty elixir.

Sitting on the curbside enjoying this saline treat, I looked again at the picture of Elizabeth Wood, or "Libby," as I had taken to calling her. The idea of running to help save a life came to me from Dr. Shapiro. He spent many years on the front line of organ donation and transplantation, and The Relay was a benefit for this cause. The head nurse at Stanford Children's Hospital had told me about a little girl with a failing liver in desperate need of support. I made several attempts to visit Libby in the hospital, but she remained in intensive care and off-limits to visitors. So I was living off that picture and the deep emotional connection of being the brother of another beautiful young girl, who was now lost forever.

I had run for charity many times over the years, raising money for the Leukemia Society, the Special Olympics, and various environmental causes. But this was different. There was a face with this cause, a child dying in a hospital bed. It seemed much more intimate. I was no longer simply collecting pledge checks, putting them in an envelope, and mailing them off to a corporate donation center. I couldn't hold Libby at arm's length.

I put the picture back in my pocket, slung the bag of food over my shoulder, and started trucking down the road once again. It was Saturday morning, so the traffic was light. Some people actually waved as they drove by. I guess it's not every day you see a guy running down the street mowing down a huge burrito at seven in the morning.

At just after 11:00 A.M., I reached Sausalito and was greeted by my family. They had attempted to hide the Mother Ship (our VW campervan) and ambush me from the bushes, but with two energetic kids to synchronize, their plan was far from flawlessly executed. Still, I acted startled as the children jumped out.

"Hey, you monsters!"

"Hi, Daddy, we miss you. Where did you go last night?"

"Just out for a little stroll," I said. "Come on, let's go running." And off we went down the footpath.

Alexandria had long, flowing brown hair, and a long, graceful stride. She made the motion of running look elegant. Nicholas took short, choppy, and powerful steps, more like a charging bull.

As we ran, the Mother Ship pulled up alongside and my wife stuck her head out. "Can I take your order?"

"Why, yes. I'll have a peanut butter and honey sandwich with a side of trail mix." I looked over at the kids. "Can I treat you guys to lunch?"

"Water would be good, Daddy. It's hot," Nicholas panted. The sun was now directly overhead.

"Coming right up," Julie replied.

We continued jogging along as our meal was prepared and delivered out the window. Casual as I probably looked, running along with my peanut butter sandwich and kids alongside me, I was hurting. Ninety-five miles of running comes at a price, even if you're in great shape. I did my best to put up a spirited front, but underneath it was an extreme concentration and focus. My mind was continuously scanning the systems, looking for potential points of vulnerability, searching for subtle signs of physiological weakness that could grow into major issues farther down the road. I was holding my heart rate within a consistent range to avert the development of lactic acid—I'd trained using a heart-rate monitor for so long that I could now pinpoint my heart rate intuitively. Meanwhile, my stride was forever being adjusted to distribute the load evenly to all muscle groups. And I was keeping close tabs on my electrolytes by frequently replacing lost sodium and potassium. One hundred and ninety-nine miles was the farthest I'd ever attempted to push my system. Attention to detail was critical. My body needed to operate perfectly to make it, so I monitored the controls tightly.

The kids jumped back in the Mother Ship as I began an ascent out of Sausalito. It was just a 225-foot climb, nothing major. That incline, however, combined with the heat, zapped me. My energy waned, and I found it difficult to keep the feet churning forward. I was hitting the wall.

Time is wildly distorted in these dark moments, and my entire world shrank to the space three feet in front of me. Nothing beyond that mattered. All thoughts were directed toward the seemingly impossible task of covering the next several steps. I've learned not to check my watch at such moments. Seconds turn to hours. You just have to put one foot in front of the other and keep pushing yourself onward. Either things will get better . . . or you'll black out on the pavement.

And this time, fortunately, things eventually did improve. The funk dissipated, the mood lifted. I'd broken through the wall.

Pulling out of the downward spiral, I found myself approaching the Golden Gate Bridge. There was a delightfully cool breeze blowing across the expanse and the view was striking, the San Francisco skyline off to one side and the shimmering aquamarine Pacific on the other. My pace sharpened, and my arms began pumping more steadily. The pain was gone. At least for now.

Chapter 15

Crossing Over

> When you're going through hell, keep going.
> —Winston Churchill

San Francisco
Saturday afternoon, September 30, 2000

Crossing the Golden Gate Bridge marked the halfway point in the race. It had taken me nineteen hours and forty-four minutes to run here from Calistoga. Another 100 miles lay ahead, but I'd just take it one step at a time.

A small brigade of friends and co-workers were waiting to greet me at the other end of the bridge. They carried flowers and handmade signs that said things like RUN, FORREST, RUN!

That they'd taken time out of their day to greet some

228

maniac on the road to self-annihilation really touched me. There were embraces and pecks on the cheek, even though I must have smelled like a moose after having run all night without a shower.

In the crowd were two co-workers, Valerie and Neil, who'd volunteered to run this next leg of the race with me.

"You guys good to go?" I asked as I trotted by.

"Yep, let's get after it," Neil replied. The three of us started off, to cheers, hoots, and clapping from the small crowd.

"This is amazing," Valerie commented as she ran beside me. "You look so fresh."

"Well, I'm only halfway there. I'm sure things will deteriorate from this point on."

"Have you talked with Libby's parents?" Neil asked.

"I'm going to run by the hospital tonight and visit them when I get to Stanford."

A local TV station was taping a special segment on the story of me running for Libby, and a reporter had visited our office earlier in the week. Neil had watched the interview. Stanford Children's Hospital was along The Relay route, and the plan was for me to visit Libby while running by, presuming she was well enough to accept visitors.

We ambled along together steadily. My fund-raising tactics were straightforward. Besides soliciting straight-up contributions, I'd invited volunteers to run any portion of the 199 miles with me, at a buck per mile. Cable has pay-per-view; Karno devised pay-per-torture. Valerie and Neil would only run 8 miles with me, but they contributed a lot more than eight dollars (they made me promise that if they contributed more, they wouldn't *have* to run the additional miles).

My pal Scotty, who'd called from the bar the night before, chipped in a few extra dollars as well. He linked up with the three of us as we reached the San Francisco waterfront at Ocean Beach.

"I wasn't sure if you were going to make it," I told him.

"You kidding? I wouldn't miss this for the world," he replied.

"How's the hangover treating ya?"

"Hangover? That won't kick in for a few hours. I barely finished my last cocktail."

I made the introductions, and the four of us ran south along the esplanade, telling stories and laughing along the way. It made the running almost effortless. At such moments I felt as though I could run forever. I'd just covered 105 miles, and the grand experiment to see how much farther I could make it had begun. Just as a race-car driver pushes his vehicle to the limit, or a pilot tests the "edge" in an experimental plane, I wanted to see how far I could go. What I now realize is that the way other people seek physical comfort and blissful well-being, I seek extremes. Why run 10 miles when you can run 100? Moderation bores me.

The obvious question I'm frequently asked: "Doesn't it hurt?"

"Yes," I say. "But it's a good hurt."

At points it's excruciating, but ultimately it's restorative. Not unlike electroshock therapy.

Still, most people can't imagine the levels of pain one endures running long distances. Most of us have run at some point in our lives and know how much it can hurt. And I'm here to tell you that it doesn't get any less painful the farther you go. Quite the contrary.

If running 10 miles hurts X bad, it might be tempting to think that running 50 miles might somehow hurt less than 5X bad. How else could someone put up with the pain? Truth is, running those 50 miles hurts more like 10X bad. Or worse. The pain at mile 40 is much worse than back at mile 30, which hurt a lot more than mile 20. Every step hurts worse than the last.

How can the human body withstand it? I like to tell people that my "biomechanics" are "genetically favorable" for running long distances. They scratch their heads and nod, even when they don't know what the heck I'm talking about. In truth, I don't, either. I have no idea if it's true. But people seem to need some explanation, because it doesn't seem fathomable to run for forty-eight hours straight.

There's really no mystery to what I do, however. It hurts me just as bad as anyone else. I've just learned an essential insight: your legs can only carry you so far. Running great distances is mostly done with your head . . . and, as Benner taught me twenty-five years ago, your heart. The human body is capable of amazing physical deeds. If we could just free ourselves from our perceived limitations and tap into our internal fire, the possibilities are endless.

My three companions kept up with me as far as Exchange 19, a relay point for team runners on the far side of Ocean Beach. Scotty invited Valerie and Neil back to the bar for celebratory Bloody Marys. I would have loved to join them, but I still had some unfinished business to attend to. We bid farewell, and once again I found myself alone on the open highway, the Mother Ship trailing not far behind.

The road turned inland, and the temperature began to soar. Making matters worse, the highway was heavily trafficked along this stretch, and a thick layer of exhaust clung to the road. Breathing in the noxious fumes was unbearable. Sweat oozed from every pore in my body; even my feet sloshed in my shoes. The mid-afternoon sun was becoming unforgiving.

Then, as if sensing my despair, the heavens parted, and an angel's hand reached out to me with a miraculous offering.

"Here, take it!" my wife hollered from the passenger window of the Mother Ship.

It was a bottle of Pedialyte. I downed the whole thing in seconds, and she handed out another.

Pedialyte is the secret sauce of electrolyte-replacement beverages. Designed for dehydrated children suffering with diarrhea and vomiting, it is the most effective isotonic sports drink known to humankind, the next level after Gatorade.

"Hey, Julie," I yelled, "when do we get off this road?"

"It's a couple miles up," she called out. "We'll meet you there."

With much more Pedialyte, I hoped.

After 2 more miles, the course veered off the main highway and onto less-traveled suburban streets in the hills above the San Francisco airport. In the Mother Ship, my kids squealed with delight at the jets taking off and landing below. They could see it all through the big windows.

The Mother Ship was the ultimate crew vehicle, and my family was the ultimate crew. Mom handed me another peanut butter and honey sandwich out the door. Dad yelled out the window that I was looking strong.

"Don't slow on our behalf," he coached. "You're on a record pace."

Record pace? What was the man talking about? I was just trying to get through this ordeal without self-destructing.

They pulled over and the kids jumped out.

"Daddy," Alexandria called to me, "play with us."

"Yeah," Nicholas agreed. "Let's play baseball."

"Okay," I panted, "let's play catch." And we ran down the road tossing a ball back and forth. A brief rest would have been nice, but playing with the kids was a better pick-me-up. I was always preaching to them, "Adventure happens the moment you step out your front door. Get outside and get going," just as my mom had urged us kids when we were young.

Well, here we were, practicing what I preached. We didn't have to go to Nepal or Africa to find adventure. We could simply lace up our running shoes and embark on a mysterious and intriguing journey right from our house in the middle of San Francisco. We did it all the time, and the kids loved it. What Daddy was now doing seemed reasonable to them (hopefully). He was just stretching the boundaries a bit beyond Golden Gate Park.

After ten minutes, the oppressive heat got to them and they boarded the Mother Ship for solace. In kinder weather, they would have lasted much longer. My kids are in good shape, thankfully—though I'd never pushed them to become fanatical about their diet and exercise, fearing a backlash. I simply tried to set a good example. Luckily, it worked. They are both healthy eaters and physically active. Watching them bound into the Mother Ship, huffing and puffing after running and playing catch with me, my heart swelled with pride.

That upbeat mood carried me along nicely for about the next ten miles, but it ran out of gas by mile 130, and a bout of despair set in. Suddenly, nothing seemed to be going right, when hardly two hours ago the world was filled with promise. The sun was now sinking below the distant horizon, and I was running into a gathering gloom. I was alone, my family having stopped somewhere for dinner; where? I didn't know. The pain wasn't just confined to my legs any longer but had spread throughout my entire body. I plodded along in grief, barely able to lift my head. Twenty-eight hours of running can do that to you.

As the pain intensified and my mood sank deeper, once again I began asking myself *why* I was doing this. The explicit answer was to honor my commitment to Libby and her family, to help a little girl in need. My struggle to run 199 miles was nowhere close to what they were enduring. It was the least I could do to help.

Of course, there was more than altruism at work. My perverse curiosity to discover how far the human body could be pushed also drove me onward. How far could I go before crumbling? This 199-mile run was the ultimate test. The proving field.

Or was it the killing field? "The natural situation for man may well be at war," Emerson wrote. Did I run because I needed to be at war with something? Or with myself? The highest form of competition is self-competition, and I was proving to be the cruelest of opponents, ruthlessly demanding more of myself, relentlessly doing battle with the road, with my own body, with my mind.

Pain was my weapon of choice.

Yet even in the midst of the tremendous punishment being dealt to my body, I absolutely thrived on the raw intensity of this moment. Beneath the feelings of hopelessness and despair, never have I felt so alive, despite—or perhaps because of—the pain.

The headlights of the Mother Ship approaching from behind shook me from this reverie. It was now almost completely dark out.

Julie spoke softly as they pulled alongside. "How's it going?"

"There have been high points, and there have been low points," I puffed. "This is not a high point."

She jumped out and started running alongside me. At my current pace, she really only needed to walk briskly to keep up. I could see the kids in their pajamas staring out the back window.

"What seems to be the matter?" Julie asked.

"Basically, everything," I said. "I'm worked. Not sure how I'm going to cover another sixty-five miles."

After a moment she said, "Don't think of it like that. It's too daunting. Remember *What About Bob?*"

It was a comedy we both enjoyed in which Richard Dreyfuss plays the role of a psychiatrist treating a patient, played by Bill Murray, on his long road to recovery. "Baby steps," Julie said, as Dreyfuss had counseled Murray. "Just take baby steps. Set your goal as that street sign sixty-five feet ahead, not the finish line sixty-five miles ahead. Just get to the street sign."

At times I couldn't understand Julie, like the time she planted a coconut tree from Hawaii in our living room. At others times, like now, she made perfect sense to me. We seemed to connect best when survival was at stake. Running until I was on the verge of collapse stripped away all of the sappy higher-level needs—delicate things like feelings and esteem—and tended to make our relationship more of an instinctual union. Pushing myself to the brink of obliteration tore down the hierarchy of needs. We somehow loved each other more fiercely at these times, when primitive emotion was the main driving force. The goal was to get me to the finish line, alive. Simple. Straightforward. More powerful than you could ever imagine.

My cell phone rang. It was LeAnn Wood, Libby's mom, calling from Stanford Children's Hospital.

"I have good news," she said. "Libby is doing better. She's asleep right now, and the doctors say that if she gets a good night's rest we can meet you at the finish in Santa Cruz."

"Nothing would make me happier," I told her.

With my vow to meet Libby and her family at the finish, my pace suddenly quickened. I could feel a tingling sensation in my muscles, as if my blood was once again flowing. The endorphins were kicking in. I was pulling out of the low. Sometimes you've got to go through hell to get to heaven.

Baby steps, I kept reminding myself as I ran along, *baby steps.*

It was after 2:00 A.M. on this second night of running when I reached Stanford Children's Hospital. *Probably best not to stop at this hour. They might have me arrested, or taken in for testing. I'll be seeing Libby and her family tomorrow anyway. Right?*

The Mother Ship was hunkered down for sleep somewhere behind me, and I trotted along in the darkness alone. At the next intersection, oddly, I nearly ran into a young man out for a walk. He was nattily dressed, if somewhat disheveled; what was he doing out for a stroll at two in the morning? From the look he gave me, I could see he was just as puzzled by my presence in running gear. Then I noticed the lipstick marks all over his face and neck . . . ah, a young Romeo exiting a nearby club with a warm send-off.

"You're out jogging pretty late," he said, stirring the silence. "What time'd you start?"

Not anticipating seeing anyone out here, I looked at my watch. "Ah . . . let's see: today's Sunday, yesterday was Saturday . . . oh, a couple days ago."

He blinked. "Where are you headed?"

"Well," I responded slowly, "I'm trying to get to Santa Cruz."

"Santa Cruz! That's fifty miles from here!"

"I know it's a long way," I said. "We'll see how it goes."

"Why are you doing this?"

"I'm going to meet a little girl and her family." The light turned green. "Take it easy."

"Yeah." He waved, still staring at me inquisitively. "You, too."

Onward I continued, my thumping footsteps gradually becoming the only audible sound. The next hour was run with a mounting fatigue. I tried to remain alert, but the two nights without sleep and 155 miles of continuous running were catching up with me. My pupils grew so heavy that I couldn't focus. Everything was blurry, like opening your eyes underwater. I continued striding forward, my eyelids becoming heavier and heavier with every step. Then came an eerie calm . . .

Being awakened in the middle of the night by a loud noise is unsettling, especially when you're running. In this case, a blasting horn jolted me out of slumber. It took a split second to realize what had happened, but the flashing headlights quickly solved the puzzle. I'd fallen asleep while running. And apparently I had continued sleeprunning merrily along into the middle of the highway. Now I was about to be run over.

As the headlights bore down on me, I instinctively flung myself into the hedges like a human cannonball. The landing was rough, but the alternative would have been much worse.

Shaken—Jeeze, I'd been sleeprunning down a highway!—I decided it was time to take a break. Crawling with wobbly legs out of the bushes, I wiped off the debris from my body and sat down on the curb.

Unfortunately, sitting down wasn't all that rejuvenating. It was as though my system had adapted to running constantly, and stopping was a foreign state of being. Pain flared through every inch of my body. I had to get up and keep going—it hurt too much to sit still.

There was one slight problem, however. I couldn't stand up. My body was simply too weak and ravaged. I made several attempts and failed each time, just couldn't get up the momentum. It was hopeless. I was done. Cooked. Entirely spent.

The notion of my covering another forty-five miles seemed a desperately forlorn hope. I couldn't even get off the curb—how would I possibly run another 45 miles? The weight of this realization crushed me. Sure, I'd run 155 miles nonstop, no small accomplishment. But I'd fallen short of my goal. Succumbing to defeat is devastating to me. Rationalizations never worked.

What to do now? The Mother Ship crew was down for the night and wouldn't come across me until tomorrow morning. By that time I'd be incoherent. I thought about dialing 911. Surely over the years the police have encountered similar situations. Or maybe not.

Screw it. I may have failed, but at least I'm going to preserve a little dignity and stand up. Let them find me comatose, but standing. *If I can just rise to my feet, I'll be satisfied. Baby steps,* I thought. *Just stand up.*

It took several attempts and plenty of bellowing groans, but finally I did it. I stood up.

"YES!" I shouted, forgetting for a second that I'd just accomplished something most infants can do at twelve months. As I stood under the pale glow of the streetlight, basking in my victory, my fighting spirit resurfaced.

So I set my new goal of reaching the reflector some twenty feet up the road. *If I can just reach that reflector, I'll be satisfied.* Although the going was laboriously slow and agonizing, eventually I made it and let out another triumphant yelp. Then I set my sights on a bush along the roadside some 50 feet up. *Baby steps,* I kept repeating to myself, *baby steps.* The momentum built, and gradually I found myself ambling along in something that resembled a patient in traction with two full leg casts. Both arms jutted forward to balance my lower torso, since neither leg could bend at the knee. Then, unexpectedly, the living daylights were scared out of me by a loud voice.

"KARNO!" someone yelled from behind. I jumped in shock. "Karno, what are you doing? You look like Frankenstein."

It was my old friend Christopher "Topher" Gaylord. The cheeky little deviant had nearly given me a coronary.

"Listen, you little shit," I yelled back at him, knowing full well who it was without having to turn around, "I don't care if I look like the Loch Ness Monster, at least I'm standing."

The headlight of his bicycle illuminated me from behind and cast a long shadow up the road. "What seems to be the problem, son? A little excess mileage on the chassis?"

"Yeah, yeah. Real funny, buddy. I'm on the brink of destruction, and all you've got for me is a bad joke? Make yourself useful. Where's the food?"

He pedaled up alongside me and handed over a PowerBar.

"That's more like it," I said. "Now liquid."

"Easy, homie. Don't push your luck."

I reached over and snatched the water bottle from his bike holster. "I'm not beyond poaching at this point."

"You're ornery, Karno. What's gotten into you?"

"Two nights without sleep, a hundred fifty-five miles of running, plus I haven't had a full meal in at least three hours. It wears on a guy."

"If you were wise," he said, "you'd be nice to me. I've got a pouch of kryptonite."

"Oh, dude, out with it!"

"Not with an attitude like that." He reached into his pack and pulled out a baggie of chocolate-covered espresso beans. He held them out in front of me and rode slightly faster than I could run. As I lurched at the bag and ran faster, he sped up, like dangling a carrot in front of a donkey.

"Get back here, Gaylord. Gimme those things!"

"Be nice, Karno."

I stopped running and stood hunched over in the road, trying to catch my breath. "All right, you win," I puffed. "I'll be kind and polite. Just get over here before I strangle you."

He rode back and handed me the beans. I popped a handful into my mouth greedily.

"Thought you might *appreciate* those," he said sarcastically.

"I *do* appreciate them. Thank you. It's just that I took a standing eight-count back there. These work better than ammonia capsules."

We proceeded down the road together, chatting as

though we hadn't talked in months, even though we spoke to each other nearly every day. He had called the Mother Ship earlier to approximate my whereabouts, then ridden his bike down from San Francisco. Alexandria had told him that Daddy didn't look very good, hence the espresso beans.

The hours seemed to pass more easily with a companion by my side. Misery loves company. There were still plenty of miles left to cover, but for now at least, the prospects were more encouraging than they had been an hour ago. As we began ascending what would be the highest climb of the course, the game was still on.

Chapter 16

Team Dean

*Success seems to be largely a matter of
hanging on after others have let go.*

—William Feather

Santa Cruz Mountains
Sunday morning, October 1, 2000

Sunrise on Sunday morning, this second morning
of running, lit the eastern horizon on fire. Bright-red cir-
rus clouds burned in the sky with blazing intensity as the
sun crested the distant mountaintops. The beautiful display was clearly visible from our roadside vantage point
midway to the summit of the Santa Cruz Mountains. Silicon Valley lay somewhere below, underneath a blanket of
fog. Had you not been familiar with the region, you never
would have known that this center of technology and
commerce even existed. We were miles above the clouds.

244

Alexandria and Nicholas with Grandpa inside the Mother Ship

The climb to the summit of the Santa Cruz Mountains ascends a vertical 2,659 feet and is so steep at points that it's astounding the pavement remains stuck to the ground. My progress up this harsh incline was arduously sluggish. I took short, small steps in a stiff shuffling movement, barely covering any distance per step. The rise I'd gotten when Gaylord first joined me had long since ebbed, and we now hardly exchanged a word.

Then there were footsteps behind us, and the first of the team runners approached. He was not moving much faster than we were—given the sharp incline, it was nearly impossible to move swiftly no matter how fresh you were. As he came up behind us he muttered an unceremonious, "Keep it up."

"Yeah, you, too," Gaylord replied. I just nodded, too exhausted to say much. As he passed, it was clear why the runner's footsteps were audible from behind. The man was built like a refrigerator.

After a few more minutes of drudgery, Gaylord said, "Hey, Karno, I'm going to ride up to the summit and bivouac. I'm falling asleep. I need a little power nap to recharge the batteries."

"Go for it," I said. "I'll see you at the top."

Before long, other team runners began passing me. They had names like "Dirty Dozen," "Old Blues," and, "Just Watering Your Flowers, Ma'am." Sensing my state of fatigue, they offered words of encouragement. "You're almost there," one guy said. "Hang in there, it's your last leg," cheered a lanky female runner as she passed. "Less than a mile and you're done."

Of course, it wasn't my last leg: I still had six remaining. And I didn't have less than a mile until I was done, I had something like 35 left. But there was no way for these other runners to know that. This was their third and final leg and then they'd be done. I still had a long way to go. To them I was just some struggling, exhausted neophyte trying to complete his final leg. Which was just as well, because that's how I felt at the moment.

Gaylord passed the big runner on his way to the summit.

"Your friend's having a tough go of it, eh?" the big guy asked Toph.

"He's hurting pretty good, all right," Gaylord replied.

"What team is he on? We didn't know anyone was in front of us."

"Actually, he's not on a team. He's running solo."

"You're shittin' me. That's insane. Who is he?"

"His name is Dean."

Crew vehicles had begun to pull into the exchange area when Gaylord got to the top. They were colorfully decorated, some with team mascots or stuffed figures on their roofs. The big guy was a member of the Berkeley Rugby Team alumni; they were driving a full-sized school bus, purportedly with two kegs inside. A bumper sticker on the back declared GIVE BLOOD—PLAY RUGBY.

As I crested the summit and wobbled around the corner, I encountered eleven of the gnarliest-looking thugs I'd ever seen. The big guy, the human refrigerator who'd passed me coming up the hill, was at their head. He had on a Viking helmet and a full-length fur coat with only a pair of running shorts underneath. In his hand was a pitcher of ale. It was 7:00 A.M.

The rugby dudes started chanting as I slogged by. "Team Dean. Team Dean! TEAM DEAN!"

It was an odd moment, but an inspirational one. And that is how my team earned its name. I say *earned* because you don't get a squadron of bad-ass rugby players lining the road cheering by doing something marginally inspirational. There was a good measure of manly honor that came with that moniker "Team Dean."

Filled with testosterone, I ran down the backside of the summit with blazing speed. The pounding seemed a little less severe, and the effort running down the mountainside was far less taxing than the climb up. It would be a stretch to say I was experiencing a "runner's high," but it was a temporary absence of radiating pain, which, at this point, was about the best I could hope for.

Jamming down the mountain's back, Gaylord in tow, I was averaging better than seven-minute miles, which was absurdly fast after having run 170 miles. But it felt right, so I just went with it and didn't ask questions.

In relative terms, I'd covered five-sixths of the course. Santa Cruz was now just some 30 miles away. But in absolute terms, it may as well have been on the other side of the universe. My success was far from assured. Even in my revived state, 30 miles is no small distance, especially after having run 170.

The Mother Ship came barreling along, emitting honks and cheers and unintelligible screams. Beautiful music to me. I waved and smiled and flashed a thumbs-up, and they sped off to the next exchange.

Gaylord pedaled on as well. "Need anything ahead?" he asked.

"Some Pedialyte would be great."

"Infant formula?"

"Mother's milk," I replied. "Works wonders."

They were waiting for me at the exchange with Pedialyte and cheers.

"Go, Team Dean," Gaylord joked.

"GO, TEAM DEAN!" my family chimed in.

I grabbed the Pedialyte and ran on. The road forked, and I kept running straight. And I continued running, and running . . . and then realized after about half a mile that no one else was around. I stopped and looked back. No teams behind me, no crew vehicles. Had I entered the Twilight Zone?

Then it occurred to me that in my glee perhaps I had gone the wrong way at the fork. I'd gone straight and was on Highway 236; the course route had bent left and was on Highway 9.

Turning around, I asked myself, *What's one extra mile?* But that mistake marked another swing in my disposition. The half-mile back to the junction was demoralizing. *How could I make such a stupid mistake?*

By the time I reached the next exchange, I was in a terrible funk. My speech was slurred, and I was trembling badly from hypoglycemia.

"What happened?" my dad asked. "Where did you go?"

I could only shake my head in despair. They had set up a chair and I slumped into it, arms dangling. The kids were firing questions, but I was too despondent to reply. A small crowd of runners assembled around me.

"Are you *Team Dean*?" someone asked.

I couldn't answer for a long, awkward moment. And then I said softly, "Yes, I am Team Dean."

It was the first time I'd said it. And despite my forlorn state, it felt good. It reminded me exactly why I was out here running for two days straight. I was doing it because I could; it was my place in the world.

I wasn't born with any innate talent. I've never been naturally gifted at anything; I always had to work at it. The only way I knew to succeed was to try harder than anyone else. Dogged persistence is what got me through life. But here was something I was half-decent at. Being able to run great distances was the one thing I could offer the world. Others might be faster, but I could go longer. My strongest quality is that I never give up. Running as far as possible was one activity where being stubborn as a bull was actually a good thing. It suited my personality.

"Yep," I said, more energetically. "Team Dean here!"

"We think what you're doing is incredible," one runner said.

"You mean the men in white suits aren't coming to take me away?"

My attempt at a joke broke the tension, and the crowd began to loosen up.

"Hey, Team Dean," another runner shouted, "what's on the menu for breakfast, a box of nails?"

The crowd laughed, and I did, too. Mine went on for a while, with good reason. It was one of those rare moments in life where everything is perfect.

Everything, except for the 23.7 miles still left to cover.

Exiting exchange 32, I knew that the next 23.7 miles would probably be both the most glorious and the most hideous of my life. It was going to be an epic struggle, an all-out battle to reach the finish. The game was getting good. I just hoped the ending would be happy.

Within a mile of leaving the exchange, I found myself flagging again; the high of twelve minutes ago was replaced by a feeling of desolation. The cumulative miles were taking their toll, and I ran along to the best of my impaired ability, trying to suppress the overwhelming desire to stop and lie down.

As you progress in a long race, your highs become higher and your lows lower, and the fluctuations come with escalating rapidity. It was like squeezing the emotional drama of a lifetime into two days. All I consciously thought about was getting to the finish line, and the mood swings came unexpectedly, without warning. There was no controlling the onset, no way of knowing when a funk would strike. It just happened.

The Mother Ship zoomed by with muffled cheers and disappeared around a bend. Sweat was pouring down my unshaven face as I strained to wave.

Then Gaylord rolled up beside me. "Karno, how's it going?"

"I've hit a new low, Toph."

"I can't even imagine what it feels like to run this far."

I thought a moment. "Want a taste of it? Bail the bike and run with me."

"Now? But I've never really run before."

"It's not very tricky. You'll figure it out pretty quick."

We caught up with the Mother Ship around the bend, and before he could react I announced, "Gaylord's going to run with me." We stored the bike with them, re-filled my bottles with ice-cold Pedialyte, and the two of us set out together.

Gaylord handled the first half-dozen miles admirably but was pretty tooled by mile 7. If there's one thing that can ease your own personal suffering, it's the sight of someone else suffering even worse. Yet he kept pushing alongside me, not willing to drop back.

"Do you want to slow down?"

"You kidding?" he groaned. "I'm loving this."

After eight torturous miles, we caught up with the Mother Ship again, and it wasn't hard to convince Gaylord to end his run there. He was exhausted, yet there was something in his voice that said running wasn't entirely disagreeable, no matter how much it hurt. I had a funny feeling that this might not be the last time he laced up a pair of running shoes.

It was just as well he packed it in for now. Around the corner was a seriously stout climb that would challenge a seasoned runner even under ideal conditions. Gaylord had just run more miles in an hour than he had logged cumulatively in the past ten years. Scaling an 1,180-foot incline in temperatures now approaching 90 degrees would've been ill-advised. Not that I was any better equipped to deal with the hill than he was at this point.

The kids squirted water at me with their sprayers as I sauntered by.

"Darling, why don't you stop and eat," Mom offered.

"Don't slow him down," Dad rebuffed her. "He's looking strong." Meanwhile I was about to keel over from lack of nourishment. .

"Wait! Wait! . . ." I mumbled as they blasted off to the next exchange station, not hearing my feeble pleas.

The climb out of Felton to Empire Grade has rightly been called "Killer." At points the pitch is so severe that even walking it is a strain. My quadriceps and calves burned in agony. The arteries, veins, and even small capillaries in my arms and legs protruded under my glistening skin like exposed roots. All systems were being pushed beyond their functional limit.

The human body is capable of extraordinary feats of endurance, but it has protective mechanisms to prevent total annihilation. Typically the system will shut down before physical destruction occurs. Blacking out is the body's ultimate act of self-preservation. When you're teetering on the edge of coherence—which running 185 miles can induce—stepping over the edge becomes a very real threat. One minute you're running, the next you're in the back of an ambulance heading for the ER.

Marching up the hill in a catatonic stupor, I began to experience a peculiar floating sensation, as though my body had dissociated from my mind. All I could sense of my legs was a vague tingling sensation in my lower torso, and I floated along barely coherent. There was a pesky string of drool dangling off my chin, swinging from side to side with every forward lunge, and my pace slowed to a crawl. A complete meltdown was in progress; I was falling apart.

And then a perky little voice cheered, "Way to go, Team Dean!"

It was a stunning young TV reporter, leaning out of the side of a rolling van, and behind her a camera was trained on me.

"You look great," she said. "Are you feeling all right?"

The dribble still hung from my chin, and I wondered if she'd understand what the kids and I called caveman language. We'd developed it while I did push-ups on the living room floor with both of them on my back. It was an extremely simple language: one grunt meant *yes,* two grunts *no.*

I grunted twice.

"Excuse me?" she replied.

So much for caveman language. I struggled for words and came up with, "Still standing."

"Well, that's good," she chirped. "Can you give us some thoughts on how things have gone?"

"Ah . . . so far, so good," I puffed. "Check back with me in a few minutes, though. It might be a different story by then."

"Sounds like Team Dean is doing just fine," she told the camera spiritedly. "We'll check back with him shortly. Stay tuned."

With the camera off, she asked if there was anything they could get for me.

"Have access to a jet pack?" I huffed. "It'd be kind of nice to levitate to Santa Cruz."

She gave me a quizzical look and they sped off up the hill to scout another location.

"Where's your next runner?" the exchange captain asked as I dragged myself up into the next, and next-to-last, relay point near the top of the climb. Winded and unable to lift my head, I muttered, "Don't have one."

Brief reprieve with Alexandria
at the Mother Ship, mile 188

"Ohh . . . you must be Team Dean. We were wondering if you were still alive."

"That's debatable," I panted.

"Yes, it's Team Dean," chimed in a voice I recognized as my father's, "and he's doing fine. Now, let's get moving, son."

"I need a break."

"Our people are great runners," he proclaimed to no one in particular. "We ran all day through the hills of Greece chasing mountain goats."

"Pops," I reminded him, "we grew up in L.A."

Alexandria began misting me with her spray bottle. Nicholas, on the other hand, squirted a shocking jet of ice water into my ear. "Hey!" I hollered, chasing him around the relay station to the amazement of onlookers.

By the time I wrestled it away from him I was soaking wet. "Where's Gaylord?" I asked Julie.

"He's in the van getting some rest."

I saw his bare feet sticking out a window and began firing on them.

"Leave me alone and keep running," he yelped.

"Get out here, Gaylord," I commanded. "You're coming with me."

Another blast of water entered my opposite ear. I turned to see Alexandria and Nicholas huddled together, giggling.

"Does anybody need a couple extra crew members?" I addressed the crowd. "They're usually well behaved."

"Dad!" Alexandria protested, and then she started squirting me in the ear again.

"Get going, Karno," Gaylord barked out the window.

Man, I thought departing from the exchange, *what does a guy need to do around here to get some respect?* And I started back out onto the course.

With 7 miles left to cover, the TV van pulled alongside me again. The reporter fired questions through the open side door. My training, my diet, my motivation.

"It's been an honor to play a small role in helping Libby Wood and her family," I replied. "That's one thing that's keeping me going."

"Do you eat dirt?" the reporter asked.

"Do I what?"

"Eat dirt."

"Excuse me for a moment," I said, whacking the side of my head. The water in my ear from the kids' attack shook itself out.

"There we go. Now, what was that you asked?"

She gave me her quizzical look again. "Do your feet hurt?"

"Ohh. Yes, my feet hurt pretty bad, but not as bad as my legs. How's that jet pack coming along?"

"You don't look like you need it. Would you mind if we do some creative film work as you run?"

"Can you just focus on my legs down and not show my face? I don't want to be recognized as the lunatic who tried to run himself into extinction."

They filmed me from every imaginable angle. I figured it would save the coroner a lot of time. Then she asked me one last question.

"So, Team Dean—how do you do it?"

"Hmm . . ." I pondered. "I ran the first hundred miles with my legs, the next ninety miles with my mind, and I guess I'm running this last part with my heart."

"That was great!" she said to the cameraman. "We'll see you at the finish line." And off they sped down the highway.

Dozens of team runners began catching up and passing me on the narrow road to Santa Cruz. Few had any idea I'd been running for the past two days straight as they grunted encouragement while blowing past me. People of all walks of life passed me—young and old, experienced runners and new recruits. Periodically some hotshot speed demon, bent on turning in his fastest leg ever, would rocket by me without so much as a nod. A hundred miles ago, I might have been tempted to chase him. But after running the equivalent of seven consecutive marathons nonstop, my ego had been sufficiently tempered, and being passed wasn't the least bit demoralizing.

Until Gaylord passed me.

"Where'd you come from?" I shouted.

"That doesn't much matter, Karno. All that matters is that I'm in front of you!" he crowed.

That was it. I began sprinting after him, and we hobbled down the highway like a pair of geriatric patients trying to reach the bathroom first. It was insanity to be running so hard at this stage of the game. Then again, none of the events over the past two days seemed particularly sane.

"Okay, gentlemen," my wife chided as she pulled up to us on Gaylord's bike. "Let's come to our senses."

"He started it," I whined.

"But he kept it going," Gaylord whined back.

"Now, children," Julie interrupted, "keep it together. We're almost done."

She rode along behind us on Gaylord's bike, keeping close tabs.

"Honey," I asked sweetly. "Did you happen to bring any food?"

"I found this bag of pretzels sitting on the counter."

"Hey, those are mine!" Gaylord protested.

"No way!" I slammed back. "Once it enters the Mother Ship, it's community property."

"Whose rules are those?" he questioned.

"I just made it up right now, but it sounds pretty good."

"Enough, you two," Julie weighed in. "Neither of you will get anything if you keep acting like this."

Gaylord made it about another mile. His fortitude totally impressed me, and I was grateful for every step he had taken by my side. The kid was tough, all right, with a spirit that didn't seem easily broken. He had the makings of an ultra-endurance runner. I hoped he would pursue it, because I now saw the value of having the right training partner. Misery loves company.

He and Julie climbed aboard the Mother Ship and it

drove off, leaving me running alone, and largely no longer at the controls. My body was now on autopilot. At moments like these, the slightest physical or mental countercurrent can have seriously debilitating consequences. It becomes critical to believe in your ability to keep going, even if all indications are to the contrary. And all indications began turning to the contrary. I looked down to discover my quadriceps radically engorged and my calves bulging wildly. Sweat streamed down my face. Another meltdown seemed imminent.

The meltdown/euphoria cycle had become so compressed that it was now nearly impossible to distinguish between the two, as if some third mutant state of emotion had polymerized. However I wanted to characterize it, it wasn't good. I was losing control of my body and, worse, my mind. Two days of running was doing weird things to me.

Until I looked up and spotted the blue Pacific on the horizon. The beach was near. Santa Cruz was drawing me in. I thought of the times Pary and I had sat at our kitchen window and looked out at the ocean, and I was suddenly infused with hope. A hundred and ninety-five miles down, five to go.

Somewhere inside I found the fortitude to ignore the physical deterioration and keep placing one foot in front of the other. I willed myself to do so, blocking out all extraneous input and listening only to my heart.

A party was in full progress as I limped up to the final relay exchange station. With just one short leg left, many teams were already celebrating the finish. People danced by the side of the road to loud music. As I drew closer, two of the dancers looked familiar. *Holy shit, was that my mom and dad . . . doing the macarena?*

It was. The sight of my dad hip-swinging and hand-jiving with a loony grin on his sunburned mug was mortifying. Where did he learn to move like that? I felt a great sense of urgency to run on as quickly as possible.

"Aren't you going to stop?" Julie asked from the curbside.

"Are you kidding?" I responded. "Do you see that over there?"

"Yeah," she smiled. "Your folks have lost it."

"Aren't there laws against things like that?"

"We're in Santa Cruz. They could be dancing naked and no one would give a hoot."

"Let's not give them any ideas."

"Sure you don't want anything?" she chuckled.

I gave her a peck on the cheek. "For those two to stop dancing would be good."

"Can't help you there," she said, smiling. "We'll see you at the finish, Team Dean."

Chapter 17

Run for the Future

> *You only live once, but if you work it right,*
> *once is enough.*
>
> —Joe Louis

Santa Cruz Beach Boardwalk
Sunday afternoon, October 1, 2000

The last 4.7 miles were considered flat and easy—relative to some of the other legs of the route. But after 195 miles of running, nothing seemed particularly flat and easy to me. Where did this zest to keep going come from?

Running has taught me that the pursuit of a passion matters more than the passion itself. Immerse yourself in something deeply and with heartfelt intensity—continually improve, never give up—this is fulfillment, this is success.

Running into Santa Cruz, I was wholly fulfilled. Most people never get there. They're afraid or unwilling to demand enough of themselves and take the easy road, the path of least resistance. But struggling and suffering, as I now saw it, were the essence of a life worth living. If you're not pushing yourself beyond the comfort zone, if you're not constantly demanding more from yourself—expanding and learning as you go—you're choosing a numb existence. You're denying yourself an extraordinary trip.

As a running buddy once said to me: Life is not a journey to the grave with the intention of arriving safely in a pretty and well-preserved body, but rather to skid in broadside, thoroughly used up, totally worn out, and loudly proclaiming: "WOW!! What a ride!"

Endurance running was my passion, my ride. So here I was, in the driver's seat, running for two days straight, pushing the mental and physical limits, striving to be better, to go farther, to give more. Excelling at my craft meant breaking through psychological barriers and having the guts and resolve to keep trying, even in the face of inexorable pain and menacing hopelessness.

It had been terrifying facing this challenge, there's no denying it. Standing in Calistoga two days ago, I had shuddered with apprehension over an undertaking that could easily obliterate me. Yet I grappled with my fears, stepped over the edge, and engaged in the battle; and forty-six hours later I was still standing. In the world of Team Dean, it's as good as it gets.

Until a delivery truck nearly ran me down.

"Look out, you crazy-ass runner! Watch where you're going!" the driver shouted out the window.

But I was in a crosswalk. I just smiled, however, and waved, incapable of anger. My blood-endorphin level was too high for me to be irritated by something so minor as being run over by a truck.

It was nearing three in the afternoon, and the sun shone brightly overhead as the course wove through the streets of downtown Santa Cruz. A few pedestrians and shoppers waved encouragement, but most had no idea a race was in progress. How funny I must appear, beat to hell and gleaming with sweat, running down the street like Pheidippides—the original Greek ultrarunner—trying to deliver news to Athens about the victory on the Plain of Marathon. Only we weren't in ancient Greece; we were in the shopping district of Santa Cruz.

With a mile and a half left, the road intersected a popular footpath above the beach. It was crowded with beachgoers, dog-walkers, tourists. I'd moved well beyond runner's high at this point and casually floated along, beaming at the sunlit scene, entirely weightless from the neck down. How it was that a person who'd just run 198 miles could be feeling no pain was inexplicable.

With 1 mile left, my heart started racing—with joy now, not overexertion. There was no containing my elation, and I began sprinting at top speed.

The footpath continued to parallel the beach on the bluff above. Off in the distance I spotted the famous roller coaster of the Santa Cruz Beach Boardwalk, the amusement park that marked the end of the course. Tearing toward the finish, I wove wildly among the surfers with their boards and the errant beachball or two. People let out small hoots and praises at I blasted by, but their faces were just smiling blurs.

The roller coaster drew nearer. I ran toward it. A chute of well-wishers had assembled along the footpath and down to the official finish line on the beach. Other runners studied me quietly, appraising me as I came bounding in, seemingly unsure of how to respond to a man who just spent two days running.

"How 'bout a little cheer?" I goaded the crowd. "I just ran from Calistoga."

They went berserk.

As I hit the final stretch of beach, my family and Gaylord joined hands with me and we all crossed the finish line together as a team, just the way I had hoped. If my sister could have seen me, I knew that she would be smiling. I couldn't have been any happier.

What had begun as a jog through the Napa Valley forty-six hours and seventeen minutes earlier had ended with a dream coming true. Miraculously, I'd covered the last mile in under six minutes—a pace that I'd find strenuous even on fresh legs. Standing proud at that finish line, I oddly wasn't even winded.

In the ensuing pandemonium, a young child was placed before me. Her dark brown eyes were wide and

Holding Libby Wood at the finish

beaming. I instantly recognized little Libby Wood. Her mother placed her in my arms, and I cradled her fragile body. Although the doctors had said she was nearing death, to me she looked like she was filled with life.

"We're so thankful for what you've done," her mother said.

"I'm so happy we could meet here, this is wonderful."

"Team Dean," a reporter called out, "would you mind turning around for the cameras?"

The barrage of flashing cameras scared Libby, and she twisted and squirmed in my arms with amazing strength.

"She's going to be a runner," I announced, trying to keep her from wiggling free.

Someone put a medal around my neck, and they snapped some more pictures of us together. Then the questions began:

> Q: "Did you sleep?"
> A: "Just once, but it wasn't very restful." (I didn't mention that I was running at the time.)
> Q: "What did you eat?"
> A: "Anything I could get my hands on."
> Q: "Where did you go to the bathroom?"
> A: "In the bushes. I looked for dry ones that needed watering."
> Q: "What kept you going?"
> A: "This little future runner right here."

I held up Libby, who was smiling but still kicking away. The crowded laughed.

Like me, Libby had a wonderful family to support her on her journey. They had all come to Santa Cruz— aunts, uncles, grandparents—and the bunch of us spent the rest of the afternoon celebrating together and cheering like crazy as the other teams came running in. We promised to meet up here again next year—a pledge we devoutly hoped Libby would be able to keep. But the sad fact was that the odds seemed stacked against her.

As the sun began to set and the crowds drifted away, Alexandria took my hand and said, "Daddy, can we go now?"

"Of course we can, dear." I was sweaty, filthy, and light-years beyond exhaustion, dreaming of a bath and bed.

Then she enthusiastically proclaimed: "Look at all the tickets we've got!" She was clutching a full deck of amusement-park tickets in her hands.

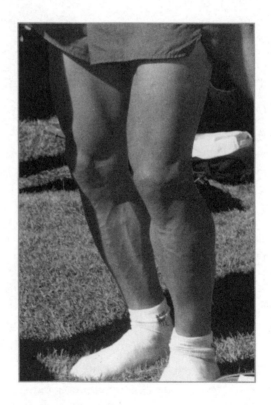

My legs after running 200 miles

"Where did you get all those?"

"Dr. Shapiro gave them to us."

"That Dr. Shapiro," I mumbled under my breath, *"what a guy."*

"What, Dad?"

"I said . . . 'That . . . *rollercoaster*, what a *ride!'* " I turned to Julie. "Hey, Mom, coming with us?"

"You kidding?" she replied. "I'm going to sleep in the campervan."

"Where are the folks?"

"Asleep in the campervan."

"Gaylord?"

"Asleep in the campervan."

"Come on, kids," I perked. "Last one to the roller-coaster rides in back!"

The three of us went sprinting toward the Board-walk, fistful of tickets in hand. No time to waste resting; one endurance event had just ended, and another had just begun. I loved it. What better way to spend our Sunday evening; what more fitting conclusion to a glorious weekend. Brutalized, hobbling, and running from one ride to the next on sheer adrenaline, I was the happiest man on earth.

By 7:45 the next morning, I was back at my desk, preparing for our weekly eight o'clock meeting. There was a lightness in my step this morning, even though it had taken me three attempts to drag my battered body out of my car. Luckily our offices were on the ground floor; stairs would have presented an insurmountable obstacle. It would take months to fully recover from the run, but it was a good hurt.

I was now working in the marketing department of a software company. Ron from the research department approached my desk. "Can you help me move these tables around? I've got a client coming in at nine."

"Sure." I pried myself up entirely by arm strength.

"You all right?" he asked.

"Yeah, just a little sore."

"Weekend-warrior syndrome?"

"You could say that."

Back to work the next morning

"Softball? I threw my back out a couple weeks ago playing a game."

"Actually, I did it running."

"That'll do it. My doctor told me not to run. It's tough on the body."

"I'll attest to that. But I can't seem to give it up."

"Whatever flips your switch," he said with a shrug.

We moved the tables and I hobbled back to my desk. My fifteen minutes of fame were yesterday's memory. Today I was back to *Dean down the hall in the office second from the left*. There was glory in running, but there would never be fame and fortune. I wouldn't be giving up my day job anytime soon.

Happiness, though, cannot be measured in monetary terms. My job paid the bills; my running satisfied a deeper passion. Limping into the weekly meeting, dehydrated, stiff, and on the verge of collapse, my heart was fulfilled. I couldn't ask for anything more.

Chapter 18

The Gift of Life

Runs end. Running doesn't.

—Unknown runner

2000–2004

A week after The Relay, a miracle occurred. Libby received her organ transplant. She had run the race of her life, and she had won.

Playing a small role in helping to save Libby was one of the most enriching accomplishments of my life. If I could use my running to benefit others, it gave new meaning to the pursuit. I wanted to do more.

I ran The Relay solo again the subsequent year, this time for a little boy named David Mehran who, like Libby, needed a liver transplant. Despite improbable odds, young David also received the gift of life a week after The Relay. I wanted to run more.

The next challenge was even grander. Valeria Caster-jon-Sanchez was just six weeks old and suffered from a failing heart. The probability of her surviving was very poor. My only recourse was to try harder, to push even farther. So after running 200 continuous miles to complete The Relay, I turned around and ran an additional marathon, making the entire journey 226.2 miles. My toughest challenge to date.

Libby Wood, post-transplant

A week passed after The Relay. No change. Two weeks passed, still nothing. Three weeks, only despair. The magic that had astounded us in previous years seemed gone. Valeria was slipping away.

Then, on the fourth week after The Relay, it happened. Valeria received a new heart.

That string of miraculous outcomes left me with an eerie sense of providence, as if it were somehow my calling to be involved. I'm not getting saccharine here, and believe me, I'd probably be running like a wildman no matter what, but thinking about my sister, and being able to help others, has given me a greater sense of purpose; it has allowed me to think of something, someone other than myself, in what can often be a solitary and selfish sport.

Yet there are no free rides. Just like the loneliness and desolation long-distance running can inflict upon a family, organ donation presents a similar conundrum. Dr. Shapiro, who has become a dear friend, once said to me, "The gift of life is always bittersweet," meaning that with organ donation, for one life to be saved, another must slip away.

The weight of this paradox troubled me for some time—until I met Greg Osterman. Greg exuded energy from every pore, as if each second of his life was a precious gift meant to be savored and lived to its fullest.

We ran across the Golden Gate Bridge together, and I learned his story. Greg held the world record for the most marathons completed, *post–heart transplant*. He had finished a remarkable eight marathons after receiving a new heart, and he was gunning for more. Yet he hadn't always been a runner—quite the opposite, actually.

A commercial plumber, Greg led a sedentary life until age thirty-seven, when he was diagnosed with cardiomyopathy and eventually given only twenty-four hours to live. He received a new heart from an eighteen-year-old girl who was the victim of an automobile accident. Pary had died in an automobile accident on her eighteenth birthday.

Greg is forever grateful to his donor and her family, and he has vowed to run eighteen marathons, one for each year of the life of the girl who saved his.

The grieving family and loved ones of organ donors are often sustained by knowing that their loss has saved the life of another. Which ultimately made me wonder: Could Pary's tragic death have saved someone else's life? Organ donation wasn't as widely practiced at the time of her death as it is now. But what if it had been? Could she have passed along the gift of life to someone else?

And then it occurred to me: she did. Even if her body was not shared, her spirit was. She had passed along the gift of life—to me.

So now's the time to get back to the existential pizza-delivery guy who'd asked at the beginning: "So, dude, do you mind me asking *why* you're doing this?" I've had some miles to ponder that one, and now I think I can answer him.

I'll start with the obvious: running has as much power over me as I have over running. Sometimes, when I haven't run for several days, the balance is shifted and running gains the upper hand, and the impulse to run becomes unwieldy. But most of the time, it's a good partnership.

Often, people can't understand how running can have such power. They say it's little more than a slightly ambitious version of walking. True, running is a simple, primitive act. Yet in its subtleties lies tremendous power. For in running, the muscles work a little harder, the blood flows a little faster, the heart beats a little stronger. Life becomes a little more vibrant, a little more intense. I like that.

I also like the solitude. Long-distance running is a loner's sport, and I've accepted the fact that I enjoy being alone a lot of the time. It keeps me fresh, keeps me—oddly enough—from feeling isolated. I guess a lot of people find it in church, but I turn to the open road for renewal. Running great distances is my way of finding peace.

The solitude experienced while running helps me enjoy people more when I am around them. The simple, primitive act of running has nurtured me. I've become more tolerant, more patient, and more giving than I ever thought I could be. Suddenly the commonplace is intriguing, and I've learned to dig the little things in life, like being squirted in the ear with a water bottle by a five-year-old child. This is what running has taught me, making me—I hope—a better man.

So Mr. Pizza Delivery Dude, here you have the answer: I run to see how far I can go. I run because it's my way of giving back to the world by doing the one thing it is I do best.

I run because I've never been much of a car guy. I run because if I didn't, I'd be sluggish and glum and spend too much time on the couch. I run to breathe the fresh air. I run to explore. I run to escape the ordinary.

I run to honor my sister and unite my family. I run because it keeps me humble. I run for the finish line and to savor the trip along the way. I run to help those who can't. I run because walking takes too long, and I'd like to get a few things done in this lifetime.

I run because long after my footprints fade away, maybe I will have inspired a few to reject the easy path, hit the trails, put one foot in front of the other, and come to the same conclusion I did: I run because it always takes me where I want to go.

Acknowledgments

I'd like to thank all of you who believed in me, even when I sometimes found it difficult to believe in myself. The list is long, way too long to include here everyone who's provided inspiration and encouragement along the way—the Western States 100-Mile Endurance Run has some 1,200 volunteers, to each of whom I offer my gratitude.

Thank you to Carole Bidnick, my agent, who has been by my side through many marathons, even though she hasn't run a mile in the past ten years. Your insight and wisdom guided me, and your tenacity and fire got me across the finish line.

Thank you to Ken Siman, my editor, for constantly pushing me to do better, dig deeper, go farther. Though it was a different sort of ultramarathon, writing this book was a daunting challenge. You've been a great coach, mentor, confidant, and friend.

Thanks to my wife, Julie, and our children, Alexandria and Nicholas. Julie, you've been a source of inspiration for most of my life, and I continue to learn from you every day. Thank you to our extended family member, Valia Naumova. In caring for Alexandria and Nicholas, you've brought so much love, compassion, and laughter to our household that you're one of us.

To my brother, Kraig, and his lovely wife, Carolyn, you are the best. Thanks for putting up with my antics all these years. Some things never change. At least I'm consistent. I remain forever grateful for all the support you've given me.

There are many friendships I've enjoyed over the miles, but I am especially appreciative of those shared with Kim and Topher Gaylord, Jim Vernon, Tom Servais, Christopher Bergland, and Tim Twietmeyer. It's been a blast, and it just keeps getting better.

A special note of appreciation to Lessley Anderson, at *San Francisco Weekly*, for coming up with the moniker "Ultramarathon Man."

Finally, thank you, Mom and Dad, for always being by my side.

Food Log from The Relay

Item	Kcal	Quantity	Total
PowerBar	235	8	1,880
Slurpee	480	1	480
Pizza	4,500	1	4,500
Banana	105	4	420
Grilled chicken sandwich	520	2	1,040
Doritos (large bag)	1,120	1	1,120
Cheesecake	2,850	1	2,850
Chocolate chip cookie (soft, large)	268	5	1,340
Cinnamon bun	380	2	760
Peanut butter and honey sandwich	300	4	1,200
Burrito (large beef)	524	3	1,572
Smoothie	425	2	850
Pretzels	620	1	620
Wrap (Thai chicken)	840	1	840
Chocolate malt (large)	1,150	1	1,150
Ice cream sandwich	410	1	410
Macaroni and cheese	386	2	772
Chocolate éclair	390	1	390
Doughnut	190	3	570
Trail mix	350	3	1,050
French fries	440	3	1,320
Chocolate espresso beans	400	1	400
Pedialyte	80	30	2,400
		Total	**27,934**